– 19th Century

nce)
-1877)
-1883)

Forerunners in France
DELACROIX (1798-1863)
COROT (1796-1875)

SM · 1870 –

RENOIR (1841-1919) DEGAS (1834-1917)
ULOUSE-LAUTREC (1864-1901)

SICKERT (England) (1860-1942)

1880 –
ST-IMPRESSIONISM

ZANNE (1839-1906)
UGUIN (1848-1903)
N GOGH (1853-1890)

THE PRIMITIVE
HENRI ROUSSEAU (1844-1910)

BISM · 1906 –

RAQUE (1881-1963)
CASSO (1881–)
RIS (1887-1927)
GER (1881-1955)
CHAMP (1887–)
URENS (1885-1954)
EIZES (1881-1953)
TZINGER (1883-1956)
LAUNAY (1885-1941)

1909
FUTURISM (Italy)

BOCCIONI (1886-1916)
CARRA (1881 –)
BALLA (1871 –)
SEVERINI (1883 –)

Influence in Russia
MALEVICH (1878-1935)

PAINTERS
-1944)
1941)
57)

THE OBSERVER'S
POCKET SERIES

. . .

THE OBSERVER'S BOOK OF MODERN ART

The Observer's Books

BIRDS
BUTTERFLIES
WILD ANIMALS
GRASSES
HORSES AND PONIES
AIRCRAFT
ARCHITECTURE
SHIPS
COMMON INSECTS
COMMON FUNGI
AUTOMOBILES
RAILWAY LOCOMOTIVES
GARDEN FLOWERS
CACTI
FLAGS
SEA AND SEASHORE
LICHENS
WILD FLOWERS
TREES
FRESHWATER FISHES
DOGS
GEOLOGY
FERNS
LARGER MOTHS
MUSIC
BIRDS' EGGS
MOSSES
WEATHER
POND LIFE
PAINTING
SEA FISHES
CATS
ASTRONOMY
MODERN ART

Also by William Gaunt
THE OBSERVER'S BOOK OF PAINTING

THE OBSERVER'S BOOK OF

MODERN ART

FROM IMPRESSIONISM TO THE PRESENT DAY

---

by

WILLIAM GAUNT

With 16 *plates in full colour and* 52 *monochrome reproductions from the originals*

FREDERICK WARNE & CO. LTD.
FREDERICK WARNE & CO. INC.

LONDON . NEW YORK

LIBRARY OF CONGRESS CATALOG
CARD NO. 64-13622

Printed in Great Britain
by W. & J. Mackay & Co. Ltd.
Chatham
1528.164

CONTENTS

		Page
	LIST OF ILLUSTRATIONS	vii
	INTRODUCTION	xi
I	CONSTABLE, TURNER AND THE IMPRESSIONISTS	1
II	THE POST-IMPRESSIONIST MASTERS	12
III	THE FAUVES AND THE NEW FREEDOM OF COLOUR	25
IV	THE IMPORTANCE OF CUBISM	31
V	THE MEANING OF EXPRESSIONISM	43
VI	THE MEANING OF FUTURISM	49
VII	"DE STIJL", THE CONTRIBUTION OF HOLLAND	55
VIII	THE RUSSIAN PHASE OF EXPERIMENT	60
IX	AIMS AND INFLUENCE OF THE BAUHAUS	66
X	ART AS A CRITICISM OF THE AGE	71
XI	THE INTERNATIONAL SCHOOL OF PARIS	75
XII	IMAGINATIVE AND FANTASTIC ART	81
XIII	MODERN INFLUENCES IN ENGLAND	90

XIV THE RISE OF MODERN ART IN THE UNITED STATES 95

XV FIGURATIVE AND NON-FIGURATIVE ART SINCE THE 1940's 100

XVI WAYS OF LOOKING AT MODERN ART 108

A GLOSSARY OF TERMS 112

BIOGRAPHICAL NOTES 119

INDEX 144

LIST OF ILLUSTRATIONS

Plate

1 GEORGES SEURAT: *A Sunday Afternoon at the Grande Jatte* (Colour Plate)
2 JOHN CONSTABLE: *Mill near Brighton*
3 CLAUDE MONET: *Rouen Cathedral*
4 J. M. W. TURNER: *Snowstorm at Sea*
5 PAUL CEZANNE: *Still Life with a Basket* (Colour Plate)
6 EDGAR DEGAS: *Dancer with the Bouquet*
HENRI DE TOULOUSE-LAUTREC: *Poster Design, 1892*
7 GEORGES SEURAT: *Le Chahut*
8 PAUL SIGNAC: *Paris, la Cité*
9 VINCENT VAN GOGH: *The Artist's Bedroom at Arles* (Colour Plate)
10 VINCENT VAN GOGH: *Le Zouave*
11 PAUL GAUGUIN: *The White Horse*
12 PAUL GAUGUIN: *Jacob Wrestling with the Angel*
13 PAUL GAUGUIN: *Three Tahitians* (Colour Plate)
14 PAUL CEZANNE: *Montagne Ste. Victoire*
15 PAUL CEZANNE: *The Card Players*
16 VINCENT VAN GOGH: *Cypresses in the Cornfield*
17 ANDRE DERAIN: *The Pool of London* (Colour Plate)
18 HENRI ROUSSEAU: *The Equatorial Jungle*
19 PABLO PICASSO: *Le Gourmet*
20 GEORGES BRAQUE: *Oval Still Life* (*Le Violon*)
21 HENRI MATISSE: *Still Life with Goldfish* (Colour Plate)
22 PABLO PICASSO: *Still Life*
23 FERNAND LEGER: *Cardplaying Soldiers*
24 GIACOMO BALLA: *Dog on Leash*
25 FRANZ MARC: *Red Horses* (Colour Plate)
26 MARCEL DUCHAMP: *Nude Descending a Staircase*
27 PERCY WYNDHAM LEWIS: *Portrait of the Artist as a Tyro*
28 MARC CHAGALL: *I and the Village*

Plate

29 WASSILY KANDINSKY: *Soft Pressure* (Colour Plate)
30 ALBERT MARQUET: *Port of Algiers*
31 RAOUL DUFY: *Ascot, 1935*
32 HENRI MATISSE: *Seated Odalisque*
33 PIET MONDRIAN: *Broadway Boogie-Woogie* (Colour Plate)
34 ALEXEI VON JAWLENSKY: *Girl with Peonies*
35 ERNST LUDWIG KIRCHNER: *Self Portrait and Model*
36 EDVARD MUNCH: *Four Girls on the Bridge*
37 OSKAR KOKOSCHKA: *Bride of the Winds* (Colour Plate)
38 MAX BECKMANN: *Cabaret Artists*
39 GEORGE GROSZ: *The Robbers*
40 KASIMIR MALEVICH: (left) *An Englishman in Moscow;* (right) *Suprematism, Yellow and Black*
41 JUAN GRIS: *Table by the Sea* (Colour Plate)
42 JAMES ENSOR: *Portrait of the Painter Surrounded by Masks*
43 GEORGES ROUAULT: *Christ Mocked by Soldiers*
44 GIORGIO DE CHIRICO: *Melancholy and Mystery of a Street*
45 GEORGES BRAQUE: *The Pedestal Table* (*Le Guéridon*) (Colour Plate)
46 MAURICE DE VLAMINCK: *Landscape with Red Trees*
47 MAX ERNST: *La Joie de Vivre*
48 PABLO PICASSO: *Minotauromachie* (*Etching*)
49 GRAHAM SUTHERLAND: *Entrance to a Lane* (Colour Plate)
50 AMEDEO MODIGLIANI: *Seated Nude*
51 PABLO PICASSO: *Guernica*
52 PAUL KLEE: *Seven over the Roofs*
53 MARK TOBEY: *Autumn Field* (Colour Plate)
54 JOAN MIRÓ: *Carnival of Harlequin*
55 SALVADOR DALI: *St. James of Compostella*
56 ALEXANDER CALDER: *Mobile: Red Feather on Black Cross*

Plate
57 BEN NICHOLSON: *Dust Blue* (Colour Plate)
58 GRAHAM SUTHERLAND: *Somerset Maugham*
59 HENRY MOORE: *Three-piece Reclining Figure*
PAUL NASH: *Monster Field*
60 KURT SCHWITTERS: *Dadaistic Collage, 1920*
61 NICOLAS DE STAEL: *Etude de Paysage* (Colour Plate)
62 FRANCIS BACON: *Pope with Fan Canopy*
63 VICTOR PASMORE: *Linear Motif in Black and White*
64 *The affinity of modern design to present-day art*

ACKNOWLEDGMENTS

The author and publishers wish to acknowledge the kind assistance given by the various galleries, agents and owners in connection with the illustrations for this book.

Pls. 4, 17, 27, 49, 58 and 61 are reproduced by the courtesy of the Trustees of the Tate Gallery, London; kind permission has also been given for Pl. 27 by Sir Edward Beddington-Behrens and the artist's widow; and for Pls. 17 and 61 by A.D.A.G.P., Paris. Pls. 20, 24, 28, 33, 43, 44 and 51 are by courtesy of The Museum of Modern Art, New York, and the owners as mentioned on the plates concerned. Pls. 3, 5, 6 (*left*), 11 and 15 are by courtesy of The Louvre, Paris. Pls. 18, 19 and 22 are by kind permission of The National Gallery of Art, Washington, D.C. (Chester Dale Collection).

Thanks are also due to The Stedelijk Museum, Amsterdam, for Pls. 9, 10 and 40 (*left*); The Albright-Knox Art Gallery, Buffalo, U.S.A., for Pls. 7 and 54; The National Galleries of Scotland for Pls. 12 and 13; The Art Institute of Chicago for Pl. 1; The Victoria and Albert Museum for Pl. 2; The Folkwang Museum, Essen, for Pl. 8; The

Courtauld Institute of Art, London, for Pl. 14; The Bührle Collection, Zurich, for Pl. 16; The Pushkin Museum, Moscow, for Pl. 21; The Rijksmuseum Kröller-Müller, Otterlo, Holland, for Pl. 23; The Philadelphia Museum of Art for Pl. 26; The Glasgow Art Gallery and Museum for Pl. 30; The Baltimore Museum of Art for Pl. 32; Heydt-Museum, Wuppertal, for Pl. 34; Kunsthalle, Hamburg, for Pl. 35; The Wallraf-Richartz-Museum, Cologne, for Pl. 36; The Kunstmuseum, Basle, for Pl. 37; The City Art Gallery, Bonn, for Pl. 38 (photograph by Sachsse); The Russian Museum, Leningrad, for Pl. 40 (*right*); The Phillips Collection, Washington, D.C., for Pl. 45; Musée National d'Art Moderne, Paris, for Pl. 46; Koninklijk Museum voor Schone Kunsten, Antwerp, for Pl. 50; The Sonja Henie—Niels Onstad Collection for Pl. 52; The Johnson Collection, U.S.A., for Pl. 53; The Beaverbrook Gallery, Fredericton, N.B., Canada, for Pl. 55; Joseph Pulitzer jun., St. Louis, U.S.A., for Pl. 57; and The Durban Museum and Art Gallery, South Africa, for Pl. 59 (*lower*).

The author and publishers also wish to give thanks for the kind assistance given by Marlborough Fine Art Ltd., London, in connection with Pls. 29, 41, 42, 59 (*upper*), 60, 62 and 63; The Arts Council of Great Britain for photographs used for Pls. 39, 47, 48 and 50; The Council of Industrial Design, London, for both photographs on Pl. 64; and Miss Camilla Gray for assistance in connection with the works of Malevich and Tatlin.

While every effort has been made to trace the present owners of works reproduced the publishers wish to apologise in advance for any inadvertent failure to make suitable acknowledgment.

INTRODUCTION

THE word "modern" as applied to works of art has acquired shades of meaning not entirely covered by the dictionary definition, "of present or recent times". It is sometimes used, for instance, irrespective of date, to show appreciation of qualities in form and colour which still seem "living" and near to us in feeling, even if produced long ago. "How modern", it is said, are the prehistoric drawings of the European caves. One writer has even given a book the striking title *40,000 Years of Modern Art* in order to stress this independence of time.

The usage is of value in reminding us that modern art, in a more limited and up-to-date sense of the term, is linked with that of the past, though we have to reckon with another shade of meaning if we confine our attention to the 19th and 20th centuries. It applies to some, but by no means to all, works produced during recent times. Modern art has come to signify a special development with a distinct character. It has branched out in various ways, but it shows, broadly speaking, two main tendencies; the effort of artists to find fresh resource in their medium as a means of expression, and also to create works of art in some way related to the nature and changing conditions of modern life.

More than one starting-point may be chosen. There is good reason to begin in the late 19th century and to trace from about the year 1880 the development which has given us works as characteristic of their age, and some as wonderful, as those of any earlier period. Substantially this little book is designed to give a concise account and appraisal of the products of the last eighty years, principally in painting, though with some reference to the other visual arts, text and illustrations being related throughout. It aims to provide a handy guide for the student and for a general public wishing to get a view of the subject as a whole, and to understand the meaning of the various movements which have followed in sequence down to the present day. The general view is all the more desirable because modern art did not suddenly come into being. To understand it, an idea of the background is desirable, and this first entails a brief survey of events in art from the first half of the 19th century onwards.

CHAPTER I

CONSTABLE, TURNER AND THE IMPRESSIONISTS

IN the 19th century, viewed as a whole, art can be seen to divide into two clearly separated categories. On the one hand there are the paintings produced mainly for that new race of middle-class patrons which after the French and Industrial Revolutions had gained wealth and status. They were eager to possess works of art, but were interested for the most part in anecdotal subject-matter rather than the beauty of a painting or in the work of those who were striving to produce something original.

The artists who could meet with their requirements prospered, but others who took an independent course found little understanding and indeed much active dislike. It is an important fact that perhaps for the first time in history a gulf had opened between the artist of original aims and thought and a public with a certain amount of culture. There is a long record of protest against productions in which the world has since found greatness. Turner's most splendid creations, his late work in the 1840's, were dismissed as senile. The Pre-Raphaelites were greeted with a storm of abuse. Edouard Manet in the 1860's was the object of intense hostility in France. The examples could be multiplied, yet painters were not to be deterred from pursuing their aims in hardship or isolation, and the sequence of 19th-century movements in art shows their growing independence of thought.

It is first seen in Constable and Turner. Constable's personal and spontaneous feeling for nature and the technique of broken and sparkling colour he devised to express it (Pl. 2) must always be reckoned among the great inspirations of modern art. The effect in France of his *The Hay Wain*, especially on Delacroix, when exhibited at the Salon of 1824 is often cited. Turner's final freedom of style is exemplified by the tremendous abstract force of the *Snow-storm at Sea* (Pl. 4) or the "colour poems" of the interior views he painted at Petworth. With Constable, Turner and Delacroix in mind we may say that the origins of modern art are to be found in the Romantic period to which they belonged.

It was in the 1840's, however, that artists began to take stock of their uneasy position in society and consciously to formulate some notion of what place art had, or might have, in it. An eventual outcome of this attitude in England was the belief of William Morris that art had lost and ought to regain its real social importance, that it should rightly comprise, besides painting, all forms of useful design and that these needed thinking out afresh in terms of function. He is justly rated a great pioneer of the efforts, later to be considered, to bring the arts together in a coherent relation.

In painting, the Pre-Raphaelite movement which inspired Morris was not so single-minded. The realistic aim of being "true to nature" with which it began in 1848 was complicated and even contradicted by the desire to return to the spirit of the past. It was in France that "Realism" as an idea, expounded by Gustave Courbet, became a force with a continuing impetus. It was no longer possible, in Courbet's view, for the sincere and serious artist to paint either the classical fables which had been to the taste of the 18th century or the historical anecdotes which pleased the bourgeois of his own day. Both were dead matter. Instead he should give a personal view of the modes, manners and general aspect of his own time and in this way create a "living art".

Courbet, of course, was far from being the first artist to depict the life of his own time, but the rejection of all artificial graces and the implied criticism of society were nevertheless a challenge to the conventional Salon art, as in the proletarian feeling of his sombre masterpiece of peasant life, *The Burial at Ornans* (Louvre). He did not, however, powerful as his genius was, conceive of a contemporary style as well as a contemporary subject. This was the achievement of a younger man, Edouard Manet, and for this reason Manet is sometimes accounted the "first of modern painters".

Like Courbet, he was convinced that an artist should paint what actually exists. He delighted in portraying the contemporary scene—a Parisian crowd listening to the band in a park (*La Musique aux Tuileries*, 1860) or a popular place of amusement (*Un Bar aux Folies-Bergère*, 1882). His method, however, was what gave his subjects life. He painted with a direct touch, keeping the freshness of a sketch. Instead of treating a picture as a laboriously built-up series of gradations in tone (i.e. intermediate monochrome shades between black and white), he simplified light and shadow into colours directly applied and vividly contrasting. The subjects of his two famous works based on old-master compositions, the *Déjeuner sur l'Herbe* of 1863 and the *Olympia* of 1865, were ostensibly the cause of outcry because of their nude figures, but it is probable that what really startled and alarmed the public of the 1860's was the novelty of style.

The controversy aroused by the exhibition of Manet's paintings in the Salon des Refusés of 1863, in which Napoleon III ordered that the works rejected in the Salon of that year should be shown, gave an impetus of its own to new developments in art. It rallied younger artists to Manet's side and made clear to them the issue, which involved both the right of the artist to look at things and paint them in his own way and also the artistic gain of so doing. The painters who were later to be known as Impressionists were principal among those who felt its force, though they had sources of inspiration besides Manet and somewhat different aims.

The term "Impressionist" broadly applies to the artists who contributed to a series of exhibitions between 1874 and 1886, all but the first being so described. In 1874 a French critic used the word in ridicule of a painting by Claude Monet, *Impression-Sunrise*, and thereafter the artists defiantly adopted

1. GEORGES SEURAT: *A Sunday Afternoon at the Grande Jatte*

(*The Art Institute of Chicago, The Helen Birch Bartlett Memorial Collection*)

2. JOHN CONSTABLE: *Mill near Brighton*
(*Victoria and Albert Museum, London. Crown Copyright*)

3. CLAUDE MONET: *Rouen Cathedral*
(*Louvre, Paris*)

4. J. M. W. TURNER: *Snowstorm at Sea*

(Tate Gallery, London)

5. PAUL CEZANNE: *Still Life with a Basket*

(*Louvre, Paris*)

6. EDGAR DEGAS: *Dancer with the Bouquet*
(*Louvre, Paris*)

HENRI DE TOULOUSE-LAUTREC:
Poster Design, 1892

7. GEORGES SEURAT: *Le Chahut*
(*Albright-Knox Art Gallery, Buffalo, U.S.A.*)

8. PAUL SIGNAC:
Paris, la Cité

(*Folkwang Museum, Essen*)

9. VINCENT VAN GOGH: *The Artist's Bedroom at Arles*

(V. W. van Gogh Collection)

10. VINCENT VAN GOGH: *Le Zouave*
(*Stedelijk Museum, Amsterdam*)

11. PAUL GAUGUIN: *The White Horse*
(*Louvre, Paris*)

12. PAUL GAUGUIN: *Jacob Wrestling with the Angel*

(*National Galleries of Scotland, Edinburgh*)

13. PAUL GAUGUIN: *Three Tahitians*

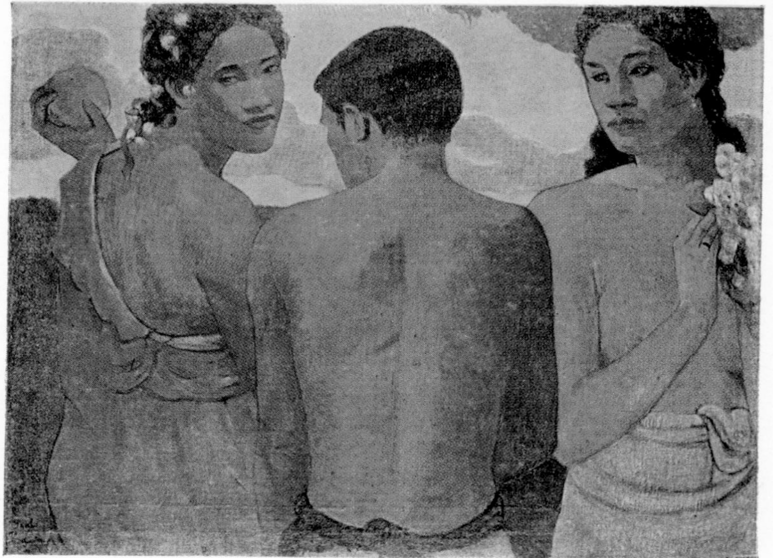

(*National Galleries of Scotland, Edinburgh*)

14. PAUL CEZANNE: *Montagne Ste. Victoire*

(*Courtauld Institute of Art, London*)

15. PAUL
CEZANNE:
The Card Players

(*Louvre, Paris*)

16. VINCENT VAN GOGH: *Cypresses in the Cornfield*

(Bührle Collection, Zürich)

it. The principal contributors to these exhibitions were Claude Monet, Auguste Renoir, Alfred Sisley, Camille Pissarro, Edgar Degas and Berthe Morisot. Monet, Pissarro and Sisley were the most consistent and typical in the new approach to light and nature which was the essence of the movement, and Monet may be singled out as the leading figure.

From landscape painting as it had been practised in France by Courbet, Daubigny, Boudin and Jongkind, he derived the idea of painting in the open air, direct from nature, with the realistic aim of gaining truthful effect. Truth was represented by light and colour as perceived in the open under various atmospheric conditions. This was an aspect of the trend towards Realism, which also suggested that one should paint scenes as they were, without attempting to pick out "beauty spots" or invent some poetic and imaginary association. Thus Impressionist landscapes often picture stretches of country or river, pleasant enough but not necessarily possessing a strongly marked subject interest. A haystack was theme enough for Monet, and in a famous series of the façade of Rouen Cathedral (Pl. 3) he is evidently not interested in Gothic architecture but in the incidence of light on an indented and broken surface. The beauty of Impressionist painting is to be found in the method of translating light into colour, which followed from painting in the open. It was necessary to work swiftly and directly and here the example of Manet was stimulating. It can be seen for instance in Monet's painting of *La Plage de Trouville* (Tate

Gallery) in which the figures on the beach in sunlight are painted with flat tones of fresh colour crisply set down and giving all the feeling of a moment of sunlight vividly captured. Yet fully to translate light into colour, which became the main Impressionist aim, made for a further step. The spectrum showed the true colour components of light and so to render it more truthfully it was desirable to paint with some approximation to these components. Black, brown and ochre were for that reason banished from the palette. Each shadow consequently had to be represented by a pure and definite colour and not as a degree of darkness, a shimmering atmospheric effect being the result.

The beauty of Impressionist paintings is bound up with this quality and the extended and subtle range of colour thus produced, though it would be a mistake to think of it as an automatic process of translation. There is always a personal and deliberate or instinctive choice of harmonious colour in the Impressionist masterpieces.

A "movement" does not remain static, but is shaped by individuals and a variety of ideas, and so it was with Impressionism. Claude Monet, who lived until 1926 and remained consistently devoted to the "Plein-air" and atmospheric aim, brings Impressionism close to us in time. His paintings, in old age, of water-lilies in his garden at Giverny on a tributary of the Seine, painted at different times of day and in varying weather conditions, were a final effort to attain truthful representation of nature. The subject-matter was now a minimum; only the essence of light and colour remained, and these works are best appreciated as "pure" painting in this sense.

Renoir painted a number of landscapes on the outskirts of Paris in company and close sympathy with Monet, though human life was his favoured theme. In *The First Evening Out* (Tate Gallery) he shows another aspect of Impressionist art; the principal figure of the young girl is clearly defined, but the theatre audience behind is deliberately blurred and out of focus, so as to render the actual optical effect obtained by concentrating on one object. Though Renoir, who died in 1919, outlived his Impressionist phase, he continued to use colour with the vivacity which Impressionism had given it. Camille Pissarro also developed its possibilities in various ways, not only in rural scenes but in such an impression of the city as his *Night Effect, Boulevard Montmartre*. When we come to Degas we must take into account not only Impressionism but another great influence on modern art, that of the Far East as first represented for Europe by the Japanese colour print.

Discovered by European artists and critics in the 1860's, the Japanese print had two lessons to impart. It indicated, for one thing, that colour had a value apart from that of imitating natural appearance. In this respect its aim was ostensibly different from that of the Impressionists, though it may be looked on as a concealed influence in their work. Their typical blue shadows, for instance (not merely pleasant to the eye because they are what we see in nature), seem to reflect the characteristic blue of the Japanese print. The Japanese also suggested new resources in composition and arrangement. A calculated simplicity of design was developed by Whistler in his Nocturnes, but Degas best exemplifies their vigour in composition, obtained by other means than the purely symmetrical balance of the European Old Masters. His pictures of ballet dancers on the stage seem impressions of the moment in their effects of movement and light, yet Degas has considered the spacing and unsymmetrical balance as carefully as Utamaro—the *Dancer with the Bouquet* (Louvre) (Pl. 6) is a beautiful example. How far art had gained a new independence in colour and design towards the end of the last century by assimilating the art of the Japanese may be strikingly illustrated by the posters of Toulouse-Lautrec (Pl. 6), with their bold silhouettes and brilliant simplifications of colour.

By the 1880's Impressionism as an art of rendering atmospheric effect had become an established style, and though its products were magnificent, artists of creative mind were already considering what should come next. Yet even when they departed from it, it was still the great springboard of effort. While the transition from Impressionism to what is known as Post-Impressionism is clearly marked, it was not abrupt. The new direction in the use of colour which it had established was pursued further, though other aims were added or substituted. Modern art was not, it may be emphasized, a sudden change but an evolution.

This can be appreciated from the art of Georges

Seurat (1859–91), who, though he died at the age of thirty-two, produced some great masterpieces of painting and many remarkable drawings. Seurat was an intellectual artist, one, that is, interested in general principles and in painting as the product of thought rather than instinct. In this respect he was very different from the Impressionists, who had never scientifically worked out their idea of colour. One of Seurat's achievements was to carry their translation of light and shade into pure colour to a logical and scientifically inspired conclusion. He worked with the rainbow colours, in a system of complementaries, red and green, blue and orange and violet and yellow. He set himself to apply the theories of the chemist, Chevreul, who had studied the effect of colours on one another when placed in relation. He showed that it was possible to produce any desired shade by the juxtaposition of small dots or patches of the spectrum components. In principle his method was like that of our three-colour process reproductions, in which dots of red, blue and yellow combine together to reconstitute a complete picture. As a method of painting this gave a vibration of colour to the eye which recalled the shimmering canvases of Monet, and indeed a friend of Seurat, Felix Fénéon, invented the term "Neo-Impressionism" for it. It is generally known by the term "Pointillism" (French verb, *pointiller*, "to dot or stipple"), though Seurat himself did not care for the expression, and "Divisionism", which perhaps more precisely described the separation of the colours of the spectrum, was the term he preferred.

The painting which most clearly displays Seurat's method and achievement is *A Sunday Afternoon at the Grande Jatte*, 1884 (Art Institute of Chicago) (Pl. 1). It represents Parisians in their Sunday best, strolling and reclining on an island in the Seine. The colour is carefully stippled in the "neo-Impressionist" manner though the observer will notice that the effect is not one of atmospheric reality such as the Impressionists gave. Seurat made a number of oil sketches in which there was more of the spontaneous open-air feeling, but in the completed composition quite another aspect of his genius is to be seen. Movement is arrested, the forms have taken on a statuesque severity, the artist has worked out a system of geometric harmonies in a way that makes one think of that Italian master of geometric planning, Piero della Francesca. It appears in the insistent contrast of verticals and horizontals in the trees and standing figures and the opposing lines of shadow; while certain curves, of the bustles and parasols (even the tail of the lady's pet monkey at the right), are repeated with harmonious consistency. Seurat thus restored to form, as distinct from colour, an importance it had lost for a long time. The studied repetitions, and insistence on line and geometric intervals of spacing, again appear in subjects which offer problems of movement. Where Degas had concealed planning in his pictures of dancers and the stage, Seurat made it a factor of essential interest to the eye in such a work as *Le Chahut* (Albright Art Gallery, Buffalo) (Pl. 7).

The influence of this exceptionally gifted and

highly intellectual artist showed itself in various ways. Monet, Renoir and Sisley regarded his work with some suspicion and would not exhibit with him, but Camille Pissarro was somewhat taken by the theory of Pointillism in the 1880's, not however, practising it systematically for long. Pointillism or Divisionism as a method is represented by a small group associated with Seurat, chief among them being Paul Signac (1863–1935), Henri-Edmond Cross (1856–1910) and Maximilien Luce (1858–1941). Signac is noted for paintings of sea and shore, harbours and cities (Pl. 8), in which he was consistently faithful to the Divisionist principle, though using a mosaic of rectangular patches of colour instead of the small dots of Seurat, and applying it both to oil paintings and water colours.

Yet it was not in the creation of a technical formula that the special value of this phase of art consisted. It marks the beginning of the end of the realistic approach to nature. In itself this fact is not to be taken either as an advance or the opposite. Realism in its various guises had inspired a series of superb works, but the time had arrived by the end of the last century when change inevitably followed a logical sequence of ideas. Impressionism had made colour important; after Seurat it became more important still, the real value of Pointillism being to suggest a new and intenser key obtainable by the employment of primaries. Equally of importance was the need to adjust the balance which Impressionism had, from the point of view of younger artists, tipped too far to one side, that is towards atmospheric effect with a consequent lack of solidity and definition. Parallel with the art of Seurat in this respect is that of the three great artists known as Post-Impressionists, Paul Cézanne, Vincent Van Gogh and Paul Gauguin.

CHAPTER II

THE POST-IMPRESSIONIST MASTERS

POST-IMPRESSIONISM is not in itself a term which defines any particular approach to art. It merely indicates a movement in time, fixing attention on certain painters who followed in the wake of Impressionism towards the end of the last century, and was invented, for critical and historical convenience, after their lifetime. The outstanding personalities of this period of modern painting differed considerably one from another in temperament, style and thought, though each in some way, from an Impressionist starting-point, initiated a new development.

In one dramatic respect, however, the careers of Cézanne (1839–1906), Van Gogh (1853–90) and Gauguin (1848–1903) are alike. Their work was done in isolation, without the support and encouragement of their contemporaries. If it was noticed at all, it was treated with disapproval or contempt. The gulf which has already been remarked on between artist and public was now wider still. The explanation of this may be found in the fact that they were ahead of their time. It was to take many years, that is to say, before others could see with their eyes. Their originality, now so well appreciated, needed an adjustment, a "new pair of glasses", which to begin with caused discomfort. If the discomfort was even greater than that with which the work of Manet and the Impressionists of the 1870's had been viewed, it was because their departure from outworn conventions was even more radical.

It is probable that their isolation was not merely the enforced result of disapproval or neglect, but answered to some need on their part to get away quietly and think out afresh for themselves the essentials of their art. In this return to first principles modern art found its vital impetus. The greatest and most influential of these strangely isolated masters was Paul Cézanne, who has been called the father of modern art. In his own day he was looked on as a clumsy and fumbling amateur—on the limited number of occasions, that is, when his work was seen in public, and except for a small and devoted following which gathered about him in his later years. From the time of the memorial exhibition which followed his death in 1906, however, his art and ideas were to wield an enormous power.

Cézanne was born at Aix-en-Provence in 1839, the son of a well-to-do provincial banker. He had a good education at Aix, his interests including poetry, music and drawing. With some difficulty he persuaded his father to allow him to study art in Paris and worked there intermittently for some years, coming into contact with the Impressionist painters and being especially helped by Camille Pissarro. He contributed to the first Impressionist exhibition of 1874 (where he was the principal object of ridicule). In middle age he withdrew to Provence, the death of his father in 1886 leaving him wealthy and able to paint in entire freedom. He died at Aix in 1906.

In character, Cézanne presents some striking contrasts. He had a passionate Southern temperament and a lucid intellectual detachment. He had an intense pride and belief in his gifts, yet he suffered from the lack of understanding shown by his family, the Parisian critics, his boyhood friend Emile Zola, who pictured him as a failure in his novel *L'Oeuvre*, and his fellow townsfolk, to the extent of enclosing himself in an armour of crotchety reserve. This complexity of character has been often described and is in a way an explanation of his art, surveyed as a whole. His early paintings were not the diffident works of an unpractised hand. They were full of ardour, confidence and bold exaggeration. He applied paint thickly, using dark tones which nevertheless were rich in depth of reds, greens and blues, and treating imaginative subjects in a dramatic fashion. In this emotional and romantic phase the young Cézanne was inspired by a variety of masters who had sought intensity of effect, among them Delacroix and Cézanne's contemporary Monticelli, who achieved a jewel-like quality of heavily encrusted paint in his imaginative compositions.

Cézanne painted in this style until he was in his early thirties. Then his acquaintance with Pissarro and the Impressionists produced two changes in his art. It diverted him from the invented subject towards the study of nature and it also caused him to realize the value of the simplified and purified Impressionist scheme of colour. He subjected himself to an intellectual discipline which grew more exacting as time went on. The study of nature became a research into the essentials of form and construction. It produced that famous dictum of his, "Everything in Nature is based on the sphere, the cone and the cylinder", and the effort not only to represent a solid by the various geometric planes it offered but to create a kind of architecture out of space, as in his views of the Montagne Sainte Victoire (Pl. 14).

The full splendour of his art appeared after he was forty. His two contributions to the first Impressionist exhibition in 1874 mark the stage of transition. They were *The Modern Olympia*, a wildly fanciful adaptation of Manet's *Olympia* in his reckless early manner, and the landscape now in the Louvre, *La Maison du Pendu*, in which, though the paint was still thickly applied, the lighter colour scheme reflected Pissarro's counsels. In the 1880's he showed a notable departure in technique, using thin and brilliant glazes of colour, almost like water colour, a medium in which he also achieved remarkable results. A great difference from the Impressionist method appeared in his perception that colour could not only suggest atmosphere but indicate also the solidity of form, each plane on the surface of a solid object gaining a separate nuance in relation to the angle at which light fell upon it. Cézanne studied these nuances especially in such simple objects as an apple, a pear, a folded napkin, the result being the many magnificent still lifes of which the *Still Life with a Basket*, 1888–90 (Louvre) (Pl. 5), is a beautiful example and one of the more elaborate. He showed that grandeur of design could belong to a plate of fruit as much as to the most spectacular effects of nature.

He brought the same attitude to bear in portraiture and figure composition. In theory he was not concerned with the human interest of his sitters, though this is not lacking for the present-day observer in his self-portraits, with their fierce intensity, or his studies of typical, stolid peasants. *The Card Players* (Louvre) (Pl. 15), of which he painted five versions, may be looked at as a study of human structure akin to a still life. At the same time, the gestures and phlegmatic expressions convey something of the essence of peasant life. It is in this unity of form and content that the later work of Cézanne may be truly called "classic" and related to the great French tradition of the past.

The devotion with which Cézanne painted in the open direct from nature in his later years has often been described. For him the Mont Sainte Victoire was a kind of still life of which he produced numerous variants. He always had the feeling, however, that it was desirable to produce an elaborate figure composition and the groups of "Bathers" of the final period were the result. In them he relied entirely either on memory or imagination—some inhibition seemed to prevent him from direct studies of the nude. The large painting of women bathers on which he was occupied for some years before his death in 1906 might at first suggest the shortcomings due to this lack of realistic study, yet further consideration shows a strength of design which is to be appreciated quite apart from any question of accuracy. Cézanne often shows that the intention of the artist or the feeling for what he is doing is ultimately more important than a display of facile skill. There have been many Salon painters who could draw and paint a nude more ably in an imitative way—but without a fraction of the interest which his figure compositions possess.

The pursuit of essentials is as marked in his drawings and water colours as in his oil paintings. Without aiming at completeness he could suggest the whole structure of a Provençal landscape with a few suggestive touches. Using water colour fluidly and lightly, he attained effects of wonderful brilliance—a good example is the still life with chair, bottle and apples in the Courtauld Institute Gallery. In the whole of his work, however, in landscape, still life, portraiture and imaginative composition, grand in form and beautiful in colour, there was also some element which fascinated artists as an idea or a method which could be taken further, rather as if he had planted a seed which it remained for others to tend to full maturity. He seems to have had some inkling of this himself when he remarked that he had not fully realized his conceptions and that he looked on himself as the primitive of a school that was yet to come.

An artist of very different temperament, though with the same intense devotion to his work, was Vincent Van Gogh. The dramatic and tragic episodes of his career have been made familiar by many accounts, though the salient facts may be briefly recalled. Born in 1853, the son of a pastor in a Dutch village, he tried and failed in a number of occupations before finding his destiny in art. A family connection with a firm of art dealers secured him an assistant post with Goupil & Co. when he was seventeen, but after some years in various branches of the firm it became clear he was not fitted for the work. He taught for a while in a private school in England and after this was a candidate for the Church, though he could not pass the examinations and his religious phase ended with grim experience as a lay preacher in the mining district of Le Borinage. At the age of twenty-seven he turned to painting and with the help of his brother Theo took lessons in Holland and Belgium. He moved to France in 1886, spending two years in Paris and then going to Arles, where he was joined by Gauguin, their famous quarrel resulting in Van Gogh's mutilating his ear. After treatment in mental hospitals and under the care of a doctor (Gachet) he shot himself in 1890 at Auvers-sur-l'Oise. He was only thirty-seven, but in a very few years, and in spite of all handicaps and mishaps, had produced an extraordinary number of wonderful paintings.

A legend has grown representing Van Gogh as a madman. This is not a scientific description and it cannot be proved—though the attempt has been made—that he suffered from any specific mental illness. His mind must certainly have been shaken by continued disappointment, loneliness and poverty from which he eventually saw no escape. Yet his letters are full of a sane intelligence and enthusiasm and his paintings show an intense observant power, a great sense of colour and a force which came from his passionate desire to convey his feeling for nature.

The stages of his development are very clearly defined. In the first period, 1880–6, he painted in dark tones and with a strong leaning towards subjects of humble life. He was much impressed by the English illustrators of the time who dealt with the life of the poor in the *Illustrated London News* (though Josef Israels in Holland also gave him an example). The most remarkable of his earlier works, *The Potato Eaters*, showing a peasant family eating their frugal meal by the light of an oil lamp, was produced in 1886, and a final product of this period was his picture of a pair of battered old boots in which, no doubt, like the English "social realists", he aimed to suggest a story of poverty. Already an unusual power can be seen, but a stay in Paris, 1886–8, produced a dramatic change of method and expansion of his gifts. He now saw examples of French Impressionist painting and was particularly impressed by the Neo-Impressionism of Seurat (see p. 9), then very much a topical subject of debate. Seurat's division of colour and use of the spectrum colours caused Van Gogh to abandon his dark tones and to take to the brilliant key of his later works. An interim stage is to be seen in his paintings of Montmartre, of which a good example is the *Restaurant de la Sirène* (1888), now in the Louvre. The full fruition is in the paintings at Arles to which he moved in 1888. This sun-drenched southern region of France brought out all his colour sense, and a particular enthusiasm was added by his fanciful idea that he might start a new art brotherhood in this region with the help of Gauguin whose works he had admired in Paris.

Once again we have to notice the influence of the Japanese print (see p. 7). It appears in his portrait of the artist's colourman and dealer in a small way, "Le Père" Tanguy, in whose shop Van Gogh had seen examples of the work of Gauguin and Cézanne. It is an element in the strong and simple design of his paintings in the South of France (an instance where it is very clear is the picture of a small pear tree in bloom), but with this went an exhilaration of colour thickly applied with vigorous brush strokes. Never perhaps have so many memorable pictures been produced in so short a time as by Van Gogh in his stay at Arles, 1888–9. He painted everything around him: the little yellow house where he lodged, his bedroom (Pl. 9), the rush-bottomed chair with his pipe and packet of tobacco, the café by night, outside and in, the blossom of spring and the golden cornfields, the drawbridge over the canal, the fishing boats at neighbouring Saintes-Maries-de-la-Mer, the postman Roulin and other characters of the district (Pl. 10); and the several versions of his famous *Sunflowers* and self-portraits, of which one of the most celebrated is that which shows him smoking and with a bandage over his mutilated ear.

This episode, following an excited argument with Gauguin, preceded a final phase at St. Rémy and Auvers when, in a sad frame of mind and under medical observation, he painted in a still more emotional style than before. He made free copies after some of his favourite artists (Millet and Delacroix), and a number of flower paintings, though perhaps the most moving of his last works are the paintings of cypress trees at St. Rémy (Pl. 16) and the plain at Auvers and the ravens hovering over its cornfields. It is an irony that of his amazing output he sold just one picture in his lifetime, though his *Public Garden at Arles*, painted in 1888, it is supposed for the room Gauguin was to occupy, was sold at auction in 1958 for £132,000.

The achievement of Van Gogh was to create an emotional impact by means of colour at a high pitch of intensity in large areas bounded by emphatic contours. One can absorb this colour with almost the same feeling of well-being as may be derived from the sun itself. His method gave an extra vividness to the appearance of an object, a person or a scene. Yet also it will be observed that there is a very personal factor involved and that the colours and some distortions of form are not solely descriptive of the thing seen but convey something of the artist's state of mind. This is especially noticeable in the last paintings of landscape with their agitated swirls of form. Such distortions, which seemed to come from the heart, contributed to the nature of the form of 20th-century art known as Expressionism.

Paul Gauguin, the third great Post-Impressionist, has, like Van Gogh, touched the modern imagination by the strange isolation of his career. Born in Paris in 1848, the son of a French journalist and a mother of Spanish-Peruvian descent, he was taken to Peru for a while as a child, later entered the merchant service and after 1870 gained a post as clerk in a stockbroker's office in Paris, making a respectable bourgeois marriage with a Danish woman in 1873. Soon after he began to paint in his spare time, his first dated picture being of 1875. He came to know Camille Pissarro and with his encouragement worked to begin with in the Impressionist style. He bought pictures by Pissarro, Manet and other Impressionists and contributed to their exhibitions in 1880 and 1881. In 1883, aged thirty-five, he took the decisive step of giving up his lucrative job to devote himself to painting, and two years later parted from his wife and family. He sank into poverty in Paris and in 1886 went to Pont-Aven in Brittany for economical living.

He now began to free himself from Impressionism. The bare landscape and rough rustic sculpture of Brittany suggested a more vigorous simplicity of style. In the following year the idea of still greater economies and perhaps the lingering memories from childhood of exotic scenes caused him to voyage to Martinique. He soon returned, however, and at Pouldu in Brittany became the centre of a group of artists, among them the theorist, Emile Bernard, and a follower of Gauguin's style, Paul Sérusier.

Gauguin had by now evolved a style of his own in which pure colour and strongly outlined forms were the constituents, as in the masterpiece of this period, the *Jacob wrestling with the Angel* (National Gallery of Scotland) (Pl. 12). It was defined by Emile Bernard (who claimed some of the credit for it) as "Cloisonnism", a term which suggested the enclosure of rich colour within a strong framework after the fashion of cloisonné enamel. An alternative term was "Synthetism", which implied a simplification and emphasis by which the artist retained only those aspects of nature which corresponded to his own thought. To regard the picture as a symbol of thought suggested a likeness between the painter's aim and that of the Symbolist poets with whom Gauguin consorted on his return to Paris. So Gauguin was also described as a "Symbolist", though he seems to have taken none of these "isms" very seriously and asserted that "while I have been credited with a system I have none".

What is clear and illuminating is his injunction: if a tree appears green to use the greenest green on the palette; and if a shadow seems rather blue, not to be afraid to paint it as blue as possible. This was very different from the Impressionist aim of representing the nuances of atmosphere. It suggested a transposition of nature and a means of conveying the sensation experienced by the artist in the most positive form, and is the key to much that has been produced at a later date. When such matters were being discussed in 1888 Gauguin was induced to make his ill-fated visit to Van Gogh at Arles. It is very likely, though he did not admit it, that the extent to which Van Gogh had separately arrived at this new intensity of colour had its effect on his work subsequently executed in the South Seas.

He visited Tahiti in 1891 and from 1895 settled in Polynesia, painting poetic scenes of native life and exotic landscape until his death at Atuana in the Marquesas Islands in 1903. The splendid dignity with which Gauguin invested primitive existence can be appreciated in such works as *The White Horse*, 1898 (Louvre) (Pl. 11), and the *Three Tahitians*, 1899 (National Gallery of Scotland) (Pl. 13), while he often introduced symbols representing the folklore and superstition of the people. Gauguin not only gave a picture of Polynesian life, he was one of the first Europeans to appreciate the qualities of primitive art, as may be seen in his carvings—which borrowed something of native style—and his wood-engravings, another aspect of that search for primitive virtues in art which has also had great consequences.

The Post-Impressionists, differing greatly from one another in character, can be grouped together in an effort to give art a firmer basis than that provided by Impressionism and a search for the first principles which would provide it. It was on this basis that the art typical of the 20th century has been constructed.

CHAPTER III

THE FAUVES AND THE NEW FREEDOM OF COLOUR

CÉZANNE, Gauguin and Van Gogh left in their wake a ferment of ideas represented in the Paris of the 1890's by the group of painters known as the Nabis, the title being taken from a Hebrew word *nabiim*, meaning "divinely inspired", invented by Paul Sérusier (1865–1927), the disciple of Gauguin. Other members of the group were Maurice Denis (1870–1943), Paul Ranson (1862–1909), Ker Xavier Roussel (1867–1944), Pierre Bonnard (1867–1947) and Edouard Vuillard (1868–1940). This group can only be noticed briefly here and not so much because of any distinctive style of art it produced, but as a symptom of the lively spirit of inquiry which had been aroused by the Post-Impressionist masters. The title of a book by Maurice Denis, the principal theorist of the group, *From Symbolism and Gauguin to a New Classic Order*, concisely states the general direction of their thought and one phrase of the author's has become famous—namely that a picture "before being a war-horse, a nude woman or any subject whatever, is essentially a plane surface covered with colours in a certain order". If you look at the work of any great artist you will see the truth of this remark; its value depends on the way it is done even if the subject is elaborate. In modern art, where subject has been less and less dictated by the requirements of a patron—as, for instance, the Church in earlier times—the value of form and colour in themselves has correspondingly grown, and Denis enunciated an idea which has been constantly pursued.

It takes one distinct form in the early years of this century in the work of artists who were for a time known as "les Fauves" (or wild beasts). The nickname was given by a French critic to a group of works hung together in the Autumn Salon of 1905 by Henri Matisse and others which he described as a "cage aux Fauves", the seeming wildness being primarily a matter of colour, and of its liberation.

From what was colour liberated? From a subordinate role as merely conveying a certain amount of information into the position of an independent force. Even in the paintings of the Impressionists, though it had grown in importance, colour was still subservient to the aim of representing some natural effect. Yet Gauguin and Van Gogh had shown that it might do more than this; that like music it could in itself make a direct appeal to the senses, and that it could convey the artist's own feeling as well as simply describe an aspect of the object seen. It did not necessarily destroy the feeling of reality, but on the contrary more actively conveyed the artist's experience of reality.

The period when Fauvism had a distinct existence as an effort in which a number of artists shared is roughly defined by the first ten years of the century. Principal among these artists was Henri Matisse and associated with him were Albert Marquet, André Derain, Maurice de Vlaminck and Georges Rouault. In their individual development they diverged at a later date, but they are to be grouped together in this first of 20th-century movements.

Henri Matisse was born in the north of France, at Cateau-Cambrésis in 1869. He first studied law, but turned to painting in 1892, working in the conventional way under the academic professor Bouguereau, and also with the painter and celebrated teacher, Gustave Moreau. He painted in the Impressionist way for a while, but by 1900 was already developing that use of brilliant and expressive colour which Gauguin had advocated.

A number of influences seem to have operated in this direction. He responded to the beauty of colour in Oriental art. The Japanese print, to him as to other young artists in the 1890's, was still a source of inspiration; and in 1903 an exhibition of Islamic art opened his eyes further to the sumptuous effects of rhythm and colour which Oriental artists obtained in works from which the light and shade of Western art were entirely lacking. Colour gained a more positive value in large flat areas than when broken up in the Impressionist and Neo-Impressionist fashion to represent an effect in nature, and to some extent the Fauvism of Matisse was a reaction against the colour division practised by Seurat (see p. 9), which neutralized the spectrum in creating subtleties of tone. Matisse set himself the task of simplifying line and colour with the aim of creating "an art of balance, purity and serenity". The *Still Life with Goldfish* of 1911 (Pushkin Museum, Moscow) (Pl. 21) is one of many beautiful still lifes in which the objects represented are set out in a decorative pattern and in a pure harmony of vermilion, pink and green. In *The Dance* of 1910 (Hermitage, Leningrad), red figures and blue background were combined with striking result in one of the most challenging of Matisse's Fauvist works.

André Derain also produced some of his best work in the Fauvist manner. He was a younger man than Matisse (1880–1954), and it was through the latter's intercession with his parents that he became a full-time painter in 1904. He worked with Matisse at Collioure in 1905, coming to share his idea that the division of colour as practised by Seurat neutralized its expressive effect and that a much more exciting result could be obtained by its use in large areas of a vibrating radiance.

This phase of Derain's work is well represented by the series of paintings of London which he produced to the commission of the dealer Ambroise Vollard between 1905 and 1907. Like other French artists before him, he was attracted mainly by the Thames between the Houses of Parliament and Tower Bridge. *The Pool of London* (Pl. 17), now in the Tate Gallery, is a celebrated example. It is a shock, perhaps, to find that the grey majesty of the river with all its workaday incident is translated into gorgeous reds, blues and yellows. You might think that subject and method here entered into a somewhat uneasy partnership and that the freedom claimed for colour was not especially suited to present the characteristic spectacle of barges, cranes, merchant ships and the distant view of Tower Bridge; yet Derain's key of painting here, and in other river scenes, is so consistently maintained that the effect is one of great beauty.

Maurice de Vlaminck (1876–1958), the friend of Derain, was another notable member of the Fauve group whose early work was much influenced by Van Gogh, and especially by his vehemence of colour. His assertion that one should "paint with pure vermilion, Veronese green and cobalt" is in keeping with the spirit of the movement. His *Landscape with Red Trees* (1905) (Pl. 46) now in the Musée d'Art Moderne, Paris, is an example of this bold emphasis.

Now that more than fifty years have gone by one can appreciate Fauvism as a phase of widespread influence even though some artists found it only a starting-point in the development of a style of their own. We can see Matisse himself diverging from it into the tranquillity and refinement of his later works after about 1910. Derain went through several changes of style in the effort to re-establish a link with tradition, painting landscapes, for instance, in cool and restrained tones of grey and green. Vlaminck eventually developed a mode of heavily dramatic, thick painting in which there remained a certain violence of effect, but from which his originally bright colour had disappeared.

The Fauve style was a kind of gateway through which artists passed into a new region of art, though what they might do later depended on the individual. Georges Braque (1882–1963), who was later to become eminent as one of the inventors of Cubism, was drawn towards it for a while as a young man after seeing the exhibition at the Salon d'Automne in 1905 and through his friendship with other adherents of the group, Othon Friesz (*b.* 1879) and Raoul Dufy (1877–1953), whom he had come to know during his early days at Le Havre. The years 1906 and 1907 were the time in which he painted Fauve pictures; "Matisse and Derain", he said, "opened the road for me"—though the road was to take an altered direction.

Raoul Dufy made use of the Fauve brilliance of colour to develop a manner, which changed comparatively little, of painting scenes of spectacle and sport, the regatta, the racecourse (Pl. 31), the concert (and in London the Changing of the Guard), colour contributing to the feeling of gay event. Yet the Fauve influence was not confined to French artists. It was very marked in Russia, where, as patrons, the wealthy Moscow merchants were strongly attracted towards the new developments in Paris, as Russian artists also were. Between 1910 and 1912 Kasimir Malevich painted in the style of Matisse. German artists and Russian artists working in Germany worked on parallel lines; they include Wassily Kandinsky, Alexei von Jawlensky, and groups of German painters whose art will be discussed further when we come to look at national developments in more detail. In England there was Matthew Smith, who for a brief time was a pupil in the short-lived school conducted by Matisse.

It is clear that Fauve art had an importance for Europe generally. As a means of giving fresh life to colour it took the painting of Gauguin and Van Gogh a stage further. What they had achieved by instinct was seen to be far-reaching in its implications. They had made colour into a great form of emotional expression and it had become a necessary step for their successors to investigate the scope thus afforded. This is not a process which we can say stopped short at any given date even though Fauvism as a recognizable and distinct "movement" was already merging with other ideas by the year 1907 and disappearing from view. The reason for this was the appearance of another idea and aim which in result was to be even more far-reaching and influential—the Cubist movement.

CHAPTER IV

THE IMPORTANCE OF CUBISM

THE search for first principles in art under all the complications and refinements with which the centuries had overlaid them was the origin of Cubism, which followed as naturally from the work of the Post-Impressionist masters as the art of the Fauves.

Whereas, however, Gauguin and Van Gogh had stimulated inquiry into the essentials of colour, Cézanne suggested inquiry into the essentials of form and construction. He had arrived at the conclusion that the basis of all form was geometric, that "Everything in Nature is based on the sphere, the cone and the cylinder", and though he did not mention the cube, it could well be assumed that this basic figure was also to be included. In his later paintings and especially the landscapes, the severe shapes of the houses, the simplified mass of foliage, the structure of rock emphasized in the clear light of Provence, showed how he applied his dictum.

Art schools of course have always had a supply of spheres, cones, cylinders and cubes from which students are set to copy the gradations of light and shade. The idea of Cézanne that "once one has learnt to paint these simple shapes one can do what one wants" would not perhaps be unfamiliar to many an art master, yet the application in the painting of nature was new. The value of geometry was far from being unknown to the Old Masters, but on the whole the 19th century's interest in atmospheric and realistic effect had obscured it to the extent that it seemed full of fresh promise in the early years of this century. Two exhibitions of the work of Cézanne, at the Autumn Salon of 1904 and the memorial exhibition of 1907, the year after his death—the latter in particular—started painters in France on a fresh course.

There is, however, another starting-point for Cubism to be found in a growing interest in the works produced by primitive peoples or those at a rudimentary stage of civilization, which so often showed a force, directness and simplicity arrived at by instinct. Such works would not probably have appealed very much to Cézanne, whose ambition it was to continue the French tradition and to make, as he said, something that would last out of Impressionism, though Gauguin was already responsive to the value of primitive art in the forms it took among the peasants of Brittany and the natives of Polynesia. The "discovery" of African sculpture was a subsequent product of the same trend of interest. Derain and Vlaminck were acquiring examples as early as 1904, and the carvings of the African artists seem to have made an impression as strong as the Japanese print had made on an earlier generation. Negro sculpture had previously been looked on as a barbarous product of savagery and superstition. Artists now discovered in it, however, one of the great forms of art when such associations and prejudices were laid to one side. The features of a head were chiselled out by the native carver into planes decisive and powerful and in their geometry it was possible to find an unexpected support for Cézanne's theory.

The two artists who together evolved what we now call Cubism, Georges Braque and Pablo Picasso, wove these threads together in their own work. They were not men of theory who deliberately set out to create an "ism" or work according to a plan intellectually thought out. They seem to have followed an instinctive course and there was a considerable difference between them, even though, in Braque's phrase, they were for a time "roped together like mountaineers". The first decisive result of the interest in primitive expression was Picasso's painting *Les Demoiselles d'Avignon* of 1907. This is not a very consistent work of art. It is of greater import as a stage in the development of an idea, for though some of the figures are European in aspect others are treated like African masks. It is necessary to look back on the prior work of this Spanish artist to see how revolutionary the conception was. The first thing that strikes one is its variety. Scenes of Parisian life after the style of Toulouse-Lautrec and rich in colour were the first product of his arrival in Paris, about 1900. These clever works of youth were followed by what was already a dramatic change—to the paintings of outcasts and beggars, austere and distinguished in their prevailing blue tones, 1901–4. The change was less abrupt to the paintings of 1904–6 when he painted harlequins, jugglers and circus performers in a similar style but with rather less austerity and a wider though still restrained range of colour. Then followed the drastic changes of 1907–9 which heralded Cubism.

To find an explanation of them one must consider the feeling of excitement and freedom which was in the air of Paris as a result of the work of the Fauves; the strong impression left by Cézanne; the current interest in Negro sculpture which incited efforts to simplify form with a like force; and together with this an increasing respect for all forms of expression which might be supposed to come from some deep-seated primitive instinct. The so-called *Demoiselles d'Avignon* was one of several pictures, of landscape, still life as well as figures, in which the sharply cut planes of primitive sculpture were translated into paint.

Meanwhile Georges Braque was arriving at results which had many points of likeness by a different road, or at least by the more logically confined road which Cézanne had pointed out. The geometric element was becoming more and more emphatic. The *Trees at L'Estaque* of 1908 converts trees into cylinders, the rocks of the background into cubes. He reduced everything, said the critic Léon Vauxcelles, writing of Braque's exhibition of this year at a Paris gallery, "to geometric outlines, to cubes". As with Impressionism, a disapproving critical remark gave a name to the whole enterprise. Between 1910 and 1912, working in such close accord that it is sometimes impossible to distinguish the paintings of one from the other, Braque and Picasso developed the idea of representing three-dimensional structure as if it made space itself visible (Pl. 22). They erected, as it were, a scaffolding in which sometimes it was still possible to see the object "embedded", as in the portrait by Picasso of Ambroise Vollard. The significant departure, however, was that of breaking through surface appearance and of showing different facets of the same object at the same time—what they "knew to be there" rather than what could be seen from a single viewpoint.

In their desire to express structure they abandoned the colour which had been the main point of Fauve art and painted almost in a monochrome. There was indeed a much more definite parting of the ways than with Fauvism. Guillaume Apollinaire, the poet friend of the Cubists, who not only wrote enthusiastically about them but devised theoretical expositions of the kind the artists themselves could not—or did not care to—put into words, remarked: "The Kingdom of the Fauves, whose civilization had seemed so powerful, so new, so astounding, suddenly took on the aspect of a deserted village." The eyes of artists generally were fixed on this new and sensational departure.

The first stage, which has come to be known as "analytic" Cubism (in the sense that analysis means the breaking down of something into its constituent parts), obviously diverged from the work of Cézanne even though it was inspired by it. He had always been concerned with the outward appearance of nature like the masters of the past. Yet the planes and segments of Braque and Picasso penetrated and even destroyed the object which the artists studied, almost like an atomic bombardment. What was the result? The observer may say that up to a point the process is clear by which the systems of grey and ivory-coloured "scaffolding" came into being; but what value have they as works of art? They are, it may be said, impressive like some great upheaval, which indeed they represent. They contain the elements of a new pictorial language. More perhaps than their value in themselves was their

17. ANDRE DERAIN: *The Pool of London*

(*Tate Gallery, London*)

18. HENRI ROUSSEAU: *The Equatorial Jungle*
National Gallery of Art, Washington, D.C., Chester Dale Collection)

19. PABLO PICASSO: *Le Gourmet*
(*National Gallery of Art, Washington, D.C., Chester Dale Collection*)

20. GEORGES BRAQUE: *Oval Still Life* (*Le Violon*)
(*The Museum of Modern Art, New York*)

21. HENRI MATISSE: *Still Life with Goldfish*
(*Pushkin Museum, Moscow*)

22. PABLO PICASSO: *Still Life*

(*National Gallery of Art, Washington, D.C., Chester Dale Collection*)

23. FERNAND LEGER: *Cardplaying Soldiers*

(*Rijksmuseum Kröller-Müller, Otterlo, Holland*)

24. GIACOMO BALLA: *Dog on Leash*

(Museum of Modern Art, New York, A. Conger Goodyear Collection)

25. FRANZ MARC: *Red Horses*

(U.S.A. Collection)

26. MARCEL DUCHAMP: *Nude Descending a Staircase*
(Philadelphia Museum of Art,
Louise and Walter Arensberg Collection)

27. PERCY WYNDHAM LEWIS: *Portrait of the Artist as a Tyro*
(*Sir Edward Beddington-Behrens Collection*)

28. MARC CHAGALL: *I and the Village*
The Museum of Modern Art, New York,
Mrs. Simon Guggenheim Fund

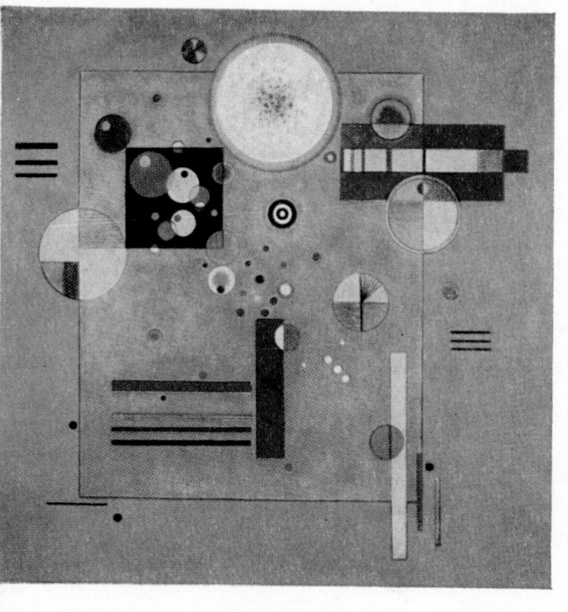

29. WASSILY KANDINSKY: *Soft Pressure* (*photograph: Marlborough Fine Art Ltd., London*)

30. ALBERT MARQUET: *Port of Algiers*

(Glasgow Art Gallery and Museum)

31. RAOUL DUFY:
Ascot, 1935

(Private Collection, England)

32. HENRI MATISSE: *Seated Odalisque*
(Baltimore Museum of Art, U.S.A., Cone Collection)

promise of things to come. Without deliberate intention the artists had launched a force which was to move irresistibly forward.

What was the place of reality in this new scheme of things which in some works seemed at the very outset to have eliminated all recognizable traces of nature? This was evidently the question in the minds of Braque and Picasso in the next stage of their work, after the first rush of experiment, 1910–12, and in the four years following. What is now called "synthetic" Cubism was the answer. This was no longer an attempt to convey essentials of structure but to assemble forms which gave the idea of reality without resort to the old method of illusion by means of imitative light and shade. While retaining all the freedom they had claimed to reconstruct objects or present them simultaneously from different points of view, the artists now made use of such familiar objects of still-life painting as a glass and a newspaper on a table-top, a musical instrument, a bowl of fruit. Their subject-matter was no less homely than that of Chardin in the 18th century, though their viewpoint was so greatly changed.

This second stage of Cubism, very different to look at from the first, was more of a reaction against it than an attempt to follow up the line of reasoning it implied. Braque and Picasso had at the outset come near to the kind of painting that we now call abstract or "non-figurative" in which forms are completely separated from the association with recognizable objects. An art as completely abstract as musical composition might be supposed a logical consequence, though other artists were to develop the idea and the evolution of abstract art is to be studied at a later date. The Cubists, however, still had an anchorage in reality and they emphasized its presence in an original way. It began as the practice of imitating textures such as those of marble or wood, a device first used by Braque and suggested to him by the method of the house-painter and decorator. His father was a painter-decorator at Le Havre and he had been apprenticed in the family business at the age of seventeen. This early experience in "marbling" and "graining" and in giving various textures to paint was now turned to fresh account. A subsequent step was the introduction of reality itself in the form of a newspaper heading, a piece of wallpaper or other actual material pasted on the canvas and combined with painting or drawing to provide an interesting contrast or comparison. This use of *papier collé* (pasted paper) became the "collage" which artists were afterwards to use in a variety of ways.

It was to some extent incited by a desire to show independence of the imitative method of using the brush alone. Guillaume Apollinaire had suggested that you could paint "with anything you like . . . postage-stamps, postcards, playing cards . . . wall-papers, newspapers". It drew attention also to the fact that the canvas or other surface on which the artist worked was, in result, of interest to the eye as an object with a material existence and not simply as a kind of window through which the observer looked out on an imaginary scene. An example of

1911 is Braque's *Oval Still Life* (*Le Viola*) (Pl. 20), oil and charcoal on canvas, in which lettering and simulated wallpaper appear. The decorative intention is emphasized by the use of an oval rather than a rectangular shape. Picasso took up the device of his friend and used it in a still more varied and experimental fashion. The cane of a chair seat, a piece of brocade or lace, a cigarette carton, a column of newsprint, became the elements of a great number of ingenious designs to which drawn outlines and stippled areas of painted colour contributed. The Cubist still life thus became a distinct product.

There is a whole later history of collage which we shall come to when considering the work of such artists as Kurt Schwitters and Max Ernst, but other factors must be given due weight in the second phase of Cubism. The flatness of forms now proclaimed the absence of any wish to give the illusion of space. Bright colour was once more employed in flat areas enhanced in brilliance by solid black. Design, as represented by the counterchange of dark on light and light on dark, developed a great vividness, almost like that of heraldry. In this form Cubism ceased to be the expression of two individuals and became a language of style employed by many others.

All the features of the Cubist still life which have been described appear in the work of the Spanish artist José Gonzales, who took the name of Juan Gris (1887–1927). Born in Madrid, he was intended for a career in engineering, but coming to Paris in 1906, he turned to painting and found a beauty in the work of Picasso and Braque to which he was at once receptive. He did not look on them as revolutionaries, in fact he described their pictorial qualities as "traditional", that is "essentially painting", even if their work was at first sight unlike that of an earlier period. "With a mind as precise as mine", he said, "I can never smudge a blue or bend a straight line." This gives a clue to his work, which is very lucid and well ordered even though he breaks up and reassembles forms in a typically Cubist fashion (Pl. 41). The grain of wood, the heading of *Le Figaro*, the wine bottle or musical instrument seen simultaneously from different angles, are in a way a formula, but one used with distinguished effect.

By 1911 so many of the younger artists in Paris were attracted by the idea of Cubism that their works were grouped together in the Salon des Indépendants. Guillaume Apollinaire, the poet-compère of the movement, published in 1913 his account of *Les Peintres Cubistes* which tried to place them in a systematic grouping, rather artifically in view of the unsystematic and instinctive way in which Cubism had come into being, yet with a sense of its expanding influence.

Cubism opened up new prospects of visual experience in various ways. It suggested what a wide field of exploration was to be found in form and colour freed from the limitations of the single viewpoint, fixed perspective and imitative realism. In the short period before the war of 1914–18 interrupted their activities, artists were busy defining the prospect after their own fashion. Some saw in it a purely geometric system of style, an ideal proportion such as that of the "golden section", between the side and diagonal of a square. It is implicit in the title of the Cubist "Section d'Or" exhibition of 1912, contributors to which were Jean Metzinger (1883–1956), Albert Gleizes (1881–1953), Louis Marcoussis (1883–1941), Fernand Léger (1881–1955), Robert Delaunay (1885–1941), Jacques Villon (1875–1963) and others. The value of geometric proportion was later to be the special study of a number of painters who separated or "abstracted" it completely from any semblance of nature. Two purposes can be seen in the breaking down and rearrangement of forms practised by Braque and Picasso, firstly that of heightening the effect of the image and secondly that of producing a new kind of structure with a visual interest of its own. These different directions can both be observed in the paintings of Robert Delaunay. Paintings of Paris and of the Eiffel Tower in particular convey reality in vivid fragments. Yet Delaunay pursued a separate investigation into the breaking down of the spectrum and the arrangement of its component colours, on the lines once again suggested by the influential researches of Chevreul. For Delaunay it had no relation to things seen but was "colour in itself that by its play, its sensibility, its rhythms and contrasts, forms the framework of rhythmical development". This effort went beyond that of the original Cubists, whose work retained a connection with reality and was soon very influential, as we shall see, in northern Europe. Another prospect appears in the work of Marcel Duchamp who introduced the idea of a sequence of movements simultaneously rendered in the *Nude descending a Staircase* of 1912 (Pl. 26). An influence on sculpture can be seen in geometric emphasis, as in the Cubist period of Henri Laurens (1885–1954) and the work of Jacques Lipchitz (b. 1891).

What may be noted also as a result of Cubism, apart from the actual works it inspired, is a new perspective in appreciation. By its concern with first principles and basic ideas it directed attention to the art of the untutored painter who set down with great precision the view of reality formed in his mind without regard to such methods of realistic representation as the effects of light and shade, or academic correctness in perspective and drawing. The most remarkable of these so-called "primitives" was a discovery of the Cubist painters in Paris, Henri Rousseau (1844–1910). The delightful candour of the natural and instinctive artist which he so signally displays was realized for the first time in the early years of this century and has since led to many delightful discoveries in various parts of the world of those for whom art is expression and not a form of professionalism.

CHAPTER V

THE MEANING OF EXPRESSIONISM

MODERN ideas of art took shape with astonishing swiftness and vigour in the first fourteen (pre-war) years of the century, and though France was their fount they spread and assumed distinct forms in adjacent countries north and south, the Expressionism of Germany being one remarkable product. Expressionism is a term of wide meaning. In a general sense it described the form of art which conveys something of the personal mood of the artist—a spiritual excitement, a disturbance or agitation of mind—and may be recognized in the distortion of form or violence of colour which results from this state of tension. Such a definition does not confine it to one period or country and it may be illustrated even by certain Old Masters. Its modern application, however, can best be understood by reference to two painters who greatly influenced German effort, the Norwegian painter Edvard Munch (1863–1944) and Vincent Van Gogh, whose work has been discussed earlier. In Munch there was the sombreness of outlook which came from family misfortune and a sense of the agony of life which he expressed in the phrase "I hear the scream in nature". Like most artists of the period he gained a direct stimulus from a stay in Paris as a young man, being especially impressed by Gauguin, though while his sense of colour was sharpened, it showed a harshness and melancholy not to be found in the work of the French master. In the main the work of Munch suggests a brooding spirit, a feeling of sombre destiny in which one may see the reflection of his own ill-adjustment in society (Pl. 36). This is the moving element in his work which has none of the serene aesthetic beauty characteristic of the French. It seems probable that it appealed to kindred qualities in the German temperament, and more especially those who found themselves in an uneasy position in a country welded together for less than half a century and ruled by a military caste. There was a wish to renew German art but with an emotional freedom that had nothing to do with the new patriotism demanded by Prussian dominance. An exhibition of Munch's work in Berlin in 1892, which incurred official disapproval and caused much controversy, made him a leader of German artists of unconventional mind and aspiration. Other factors made for a growing unrest in art which found its first vent in the group formed at Dresden in 1905 under the title, "Die Brücke", "The Bridge"—between, it might be assumed, past, present and future.

The members of Die Brücke—significantly founded not in the new capital, Berlin, but in an old regional centre of art, Dresden—had that desire to work on first principles and primal models which has been noted elsewhere. The rough strength of old German woodcuts, the primitive force of African sculpture, were qualities they sought to regain. Yet the strongest influence was that of the French Fauves and the new impulse they had given to expression through colour. Ernst Ludwig Kirchner (1880–1917) used colour flat and brilliant with all Matisse's freedom but with an added un-French violence of orange-yellow, blue and red which gives its special vividness to his *Self Portrait and Model* (Kunsthalle, Hamburg) (Pl. 35). Associated with him are Eric Heckel (*b.* 1883), a fellow student with Kirchner at the architectural school in Dresden, and Karl Schmidt-Rottluff (*b.* 1884), in whom there is still something of the German Gothic spirit in their heavily accented forms. Emil Nolde (1867–1955) is an artist whose colour moves and disturbs the spectator by its suggestion of a wild, barbaric violence.

A second phase of Expressionism is represented by the *Blaue Reiter* group founded in Munich in 1911 by Wassily Kandinsky and others and called *The Blue Rider* after the title of one of Kandinsky's paintings. The group was distinct from Die Brücke in its less definitely national composition and in the direction of its art. Kandinsky (1866–1944) and Alexei von Jawlensky (1864–1941) were Russians, Paul Klee (1876–1940) was German-Swiss, though Franz Marc (1880–1916) was born in Munich and August Macke (1887–1914) in the Rhineland. The non-national aspect of the movement is signalized by the participation of French artists in the Blue Rider exhibitions, notably Delaunay whose experiments in colour exerted a great effect. Personalities widely different were linked by a delight in intensities of colour and a fresh liberation of its energy.

Marc and Macke were both killed on active service in the 1914 war, but before it broke out had shown brilliant qualities. Marc is best known for his paintings of animals, horses and deer, though these are symbols of a delight in nature rather than animal studies of the kind that an earlier age had produced, and he uses reds and blues as in the *Red Horses* of the Folkwang Museum, Essen (Pl. 25), with a joyous freedom which recalls that of Derain's paintings of London. Macke is noted for paintings of figure groups in parks and streets forming well-knit, simplified designs but also richly glowing in colour. A visit to Tunis with Paul Klee early in 1914 produced fresh and gorgeous simplifications of colour which he was, unhappily, not to live to carry farther. The Russians brought with them an intense fervour which can be appreciated in the heads of women painted by Jawlensky. A Russian aristocrat and for a time an officer in the Imperial Guard, he gave up a military career for painting, moved to Munich in 1896 and later exhibited with the French Fauves, using green, red and purple at their highest pitch and working with a religious concentration like that of a Russian icon painter (Pl. 34).

The greatest artist of the group was Paul Klee, though in the Blue Rider period he was only at the beginning of a career which needs to be considered in a broader context. The most influential and prophetic member was Kandinsky, a Russian born in

Moscow who had studied art in Munich. For him the whole tendency of form and colour in modern art resolved into the separation of a "pure" art from any representational aim. A pure art was not, in his view, any particular mode of arranging forms and colours on a surface but a spiritual expression. "That is beautiful which is produced by internal necessity, which springs from the soul" was the theme of the essay he published in 1912, translated under the title of *Concerning the Spiritual in Art*, in which a Russian mysticism may be traced. It was written in 1910, by which time Kandinsky had already produced the first of his completely abstract paintings with no reference whatever to nature.

It is necessary at this point to consider what "abstract" implies. In some degree all art is abstract in the sense that even the most concrete picture of reality, to possess any value, must be based on some plan of line, mass, arrangement and colour which exists quite apart from the nature of the objects represented. They are, in theory, like the essential elements of music which appeals to the emotions without being imitative or descriptive of natural sound. The thought that painting "could develop the same kind of powers that music possessed" came to Kandinsky after witnessing a performance of Wagner's *Lohengrin*. The slight importance a subject need have was a conclusion he drew from one of Monet's *Haystacks*. After some essays in landscape and some illustrative pictures suggestive of Russian fairy tales, he embarked on his *Improvisations*, a whirl of lines and patches of colour.

No cut-and-dried explanation can be given of these works, which he himself describes as "a largely unconscious, spontaneous expression of inner character, of non-material (i.e. spiritual) nature". A problem arises for the observer which recurs in the later forms of abstract expression of which Kandinsky was the pioneer. By what standard are we to appraise them? Evidently any relation with external reality must be left out of account by the nature of the artist's aim. The main question involved is whether these paintings convey to you the emotional experience of the artist. It may be found in the personality the cryptic shapes take on, the feeling of animation they give, the surge and insistence of colour, the presence of a non-material force. They are a kind of rhapsody. More closely to define "what springs from the soul" partakes of the difficulty of defining the soul itself. Yet just as we recognize the existence of a "self" distinct from the body so it may be recognized in a form of art not devoted to the reflection of material things. At this point painting stands on the threshold of an inquiry parallel to that of modern science, philosophy and psychology. They take into account such aspects of non-material existence as the nature of dreams, the state of unconsciousness, memory as a faculty not confined to the physical present, the discovery of science that solid matter is capable of being resolved into abstract movement and energy. In various ways art has come to deal with these preoccupations of our time and so, as in the past, has its close connection with life. Kandinsky, in a sense taking a first plunge into the void, leads us to consider art as an adventure of the spirit.

In other Expressionists there has been more specifically a view of society, from an independent or isolated viewpoint, often intensely critical. Not connected with the Blue Rider group but outstanding in Germany is Max Beckmann (1884–1950), whose style was as hard and uncompromising as that of the old German masters by whom he was influenced, and implies a bitter sense of human brutality and frailty (Pl. 38). Oskar Kokoschka (*b.* 1886) is another painter of restless and passionate imagination who has remained independent of movements. Both these painters, however, found their full expression after 1918; so, too, did a Belgian Expressionist painter of note, Constant Permeke (1886–1952), who has painted the life of working folk with a rough simplicity. German art in the pre-1914 years showed a swift development related to that of France, harsher and more violent in its results but full of extraordinary power.

CHAPTER VI

THE MEANING OF FUTURISM

In France the course of modern art up to 1914 seems to show little concern, outwardly, with the general trend of modern life, even though the Cubists had made a revolutionary change in the approach to painting. Artists were more occupied with expressing themselves than with expressing the 20th century. Futurism, launched by the Italian poet Filippo Tomasso Marinetti (1876–1944) in 1909, was different. From the start it had a name and a manifesto which declared a purpose. It was a conscious response to the gathering mechanical force and movement of the 20th century. Locomotives, liners, battleships, racing cars, the quick jerky motion of the silent film, inspired an enthusiasm which was expressed in fiery general terms by Marinetti and later by his artist followers in more specific reference to painting and sculpture.

It was also the first attempt to unite the arts in outlook and tempo. Poetry and music were to be allied to painting and sculpture in "dynamism", the interpretation and praise of mechanical force. From each art all reminders of the past were to be excluded and the past was to be buried in oblivion. If one asks why this worship of machinery and hatred of the past should grow up in Italy especially, a reason may be found in the extent to which Italy was a poor and undeveloped country and also a country overshadowed by a great history in art. "We would deliver Italy", said Marinetti, "from its canker of professors, archaeologists, cicerones and antiquaries . . . free her from the numberless museums which cover her with as many cemeteries." There was, in the original manifesto, a good deal of absurd and provocative stuff, glorifying war, contempt for women and so on, but if one leaves all this on one side, there remains the potentially fruitful idea that original art interprets the present and does not merely imitate what previous ages have achieved. In this endeavour the leading spirit was Umberto Boccioni (1882–1916), together with Giacomo Balla (1871–1958), Carlo Carrà (*b.* 1881), Luigi Russolo (1885–1947) and Gino Severini (*b.* 1883). In the Cubist paintings of Paris they found a ready-made means of giving their ideas shape. The intersecting planes and angles of Cubism were used with effect to convey the successive and overlapping sensations produced by the movement of players on a football field or dancers in a cabaret, a sequence of images in time and space which the Futurists sought simultaneously to present.

An elementary way of representing motion is to be seen in the celebrated *Dog on a Leash* by Balla (Museum of Modern Art, New York) (Pl. 24), in which, basically, he resorts to the simple caricaturist's device of drawing a series of wavy lines to indicate the wagging of a dog's tail. The employment of the Cubist method of analysis is a rather different thing, as exemplified by the French artist Marcel Duchamp in the *Nude descending a Staircase* already referred to (p. 42), which gives a more abstract presentation of movement in time and space. The attempt to convey speed results in excluding the recognizable object altogether and suggesting rushing movement in the arrow-like and curving shapes of Russolo and Balla. Duchamp clearly explains this tendency in saying: "If I show the ascent of an aeroplane, I try to show what it does. I do not make a still-life picture of it." Boccioni's effort to convey "not the construction of bodies but the construction of the action of the bodies" in the static art of sculpture is one of the most striking aspects of the movement.

Futurism did not last long. Boccioni, its most creative personality, was killed in a riding accident in 1916. Other artists quietly seceded from the movement. As a programme of militant modernization it was superseded by Fascism after the 1914–18 war and has since shared its unpopularity among peace-loving democracies. Yet its products and its influence were far from negligible. The film was able to represent motion and speed much more effectively than a painting; yet in their efforts to symbolize this energy, the Futurists used the geometric forms of Cubism and the device of presenting different aspects of an object simultaneously with conspicuous skill. Though in theory opposed to Cubism, in fact they popularized many of its distinguishing features, and the challenging assertions of their manifestos and Marinetti's missionary visits and exhibitions abroad had their result. "Cubo-Futurism", as it may be called, had a notable exponent in pre-1914 Russia in Kasimir Malevich (1878–1935), and, apart from pictorial style, the Futurist insistence that art should keep pace with the progress and growth of the modern world kindled an enthusiasm in Russia which was to give rise to further extraordinary developments.

In conservative England, which had as yet barely grown accustomed to Impressionist painting, all the Continental developments so far described provoked much hostile feeling. The Post-Impressionist exhibitions organized by Roger Fry, 1910–11 and 1912, had seemed outrageous, still more perhaps the Futurist Exhibition held in London in 1913, in which painting and sculpture were partnered by readings of the staccato free verse of Marinetti and other Futurist poets and expositions of the *Art of Noises* by Luigi Russolo. A few artists, however, responded to these alien excitements. C. R. W. Nevinson (1889–1946) for a while used the language of Cubo-Futurism and his paintings of the Western Front, full of dynamic tension, bring the theories of Futurism dramatically face to face with grim reality. Vorticism, the only English contribution to the growing list of movements, was a version of Futurism revised by Wyndham Lewis (1884–1957) and principally represented by his work, in which he shows the attachment to hard and machine-like forms, though rejecting the aim of rendering movement and leaving himself latitude for some imaginative association (Pl. 27).

Related to Futurism in tendency is the work of one of the most distinguished modern French artists, Fernand Léger (1881–1955). Originally trained as an architect, he turned to painting and was impressed in turn by the neo-Impressionism of Signac, the Fauve colour of Matisse and the Cubism of Picasso and Braque. Cubism provided the basis of his style but Léger's approach was greatly affected by his period of service in the French army. Like the Futurists he became interested in the mechanical forms of armoured cars and big guns, and viewing the war generally as a mechanical operation, he could see even the *poilus* in the trenches as robot men whose arms and fingers became cylinders articulated like the forms of the machine (Pl. 23).

Thus, after the war, Léger became interested, by a natural transition, in all the background of modern industrial civilization, its signs, constructions and typical objects. Though later he returned to paintings with popular human themes, the main value of his work is to be found in its design, that is to say, an ordered simplification of shapes which appeals to the eye by virtue of this quality. It was a faculty which enabled him to turn successfully to design in a number of forms: for an experimental film (*Ballet Mécanique*, 1923–4), for the theatre, for stained glass and mosaic. His aims are related to those of others who in the 1920's looked for some means of relating the explorations of the painter to productions in other media and of giving them a more direct relation than hitherto with modern life. The Futurists had suggested this in a rather wild and romantic way. The idea was now applied elsewhere with a greater sense of practical purpose. The fanciful relation with dynamic movement was replaced by ideas of a relation with architecture.

To purify and simplify form in architecture and all the arts connected with it was the aim of the Swiss architect, painter, designer and writer Le Corbusier (Charles Edouard Jeanneret, *b.* 1887). His ideal was a rational and functional architecture, not borrowing "styles" from the past but answering to modern needs. The intention is expressed in his famous phrase that a house is "a machine for living in". A manifesto published in 1918 by Le Corbusier and the painter Amédée Ozenfant (*b.* 1886) proposed that Cubism should be purified of the tendency to become merely a picturesque studio product and given a more precise architectural form. Léger was associated with them in this venture, the basic assumption being that a new age required a new art just as much as new developments in science and industry. A parallel with this "new spirit" in France was the important movement in Holland known as "De Stijl" ("Style").

CHAPTER VII

"DE STIJL", THE CONTRIBUTION OF HOLLAND

De Stijl was the name given to the publication started in 1917 by Theo van Doesburg, a theorist and painter, and subsequently applied to the group of architects and painters who subscribed to its ideas. The movement kept some organized existence until *c.*1930. It sought for the comprehensive term which would bring the arts into a consistent and ordered relation. "A new plastic beauty", according to van Doesburg, was to be that of "pure thought in which no image based on phenomena is involved but where numbers, measurements and abstract line have occupied its place." This in practice meant the use of rectangular forms and horizontal and vertical lines which excluded all irregularities and accidents. The rectangle was favoured as a form devised by man and furthest from the disorder of nature. You might think this a cold and inhuman doctrine as applied to art and a surprising one to come from a country which had produced so thoroughly human a genius as Rembrandt and had in the past taken such delight in pictures full of natural detail, picturesque landscapes, interiors of houses, flowers, fruit and so on.

On the other hand it has been pointed out that the Dutch have developed a very strict sense of order. As a result of their constant battle with sea and flood their level lands have become the "least natural of European landscapes", geometrically planned with dykes and sea-walls. The puritan character of the northern Netherlands, it has also been said, made the idea of simplifying and "purifying" art especially appealing. But what must also be taken into account is the fact that architecture had a prominent place in the movement and that the need felt to find a common ground for architecture and the arts of design made it necessary to dispense with the traditional ideas of the picture painter. If you wanted to find a principle of design capable of being applied to a house and its furniture, the plan of a town or even the layout of a page of type, evidently you would have to resort to some very general basis and this is what De Stijl proposed.

Painting, however, was a principal means of giving visual form to the idea. The leading De Stijl painter was Piet Mondrian (originally Mondriaan) (1872–1944). First trained in Holland, he stayed in Paris between 1911 and 1914, being much influenced by the analytical Cubism of Picasso and Braque, the "breaking down" of reality into its main directions and constituents of form. There is a series of paintings of trees by him, produced between 1910 and 1912, which gives an interesting demonstration of stages in the process of "abstracting" these elements from a nature study.

Yet his work in the years following has a different starting-point. Instead of evolving a design from natural forms, he begins with the already determined forms of squares and straight lines in measured proportion. They do not attempt to represent anything. The colour that fills in the rectangles is absolutely flat and without shading or modification, a little like a panel of stained glass. This is more accurately called "non-representational" or "non-figurative" art rather than abstract and is carried to an uncompromising extreme which many people find hard to appreciate. A painting in which his thought is perhaps easiest to follow is one of his less austere productions, his *Broadway Boogie-Woogie* (Pl. 33), an intricate arrangement of rectangles like a street plan and with a lively counterchange of different colours in small squares placed at varying intervals of distance, suggesting something of the tempo of life in New York.

It will have been seen that the De Stijl movement

was intended to be comprehensive. It sought to devise a kind of universal language, an Esperanto of art, valid anywhere and in many kinds of application. How far did it succeed in its purpose? Do the paintings of van Doesburg, Piet Mondrian and Bart van der Leck create the intended "new beauty"? To some they will seem too rigid and drastically simplified to convey all that philosophic enthusiasm which fermented in the minds of their producers. Yet in other ways the value of their ideas can be more exactly assessed. Architecture stood in want of the simplifying process which would get rid of the confused welter of styles left over from the past and lend itself to modern needs and modern methods of construction. The De Stijl architects have been influential. J. J. P. Oud (*b.* 1890), who was made city architect of Rotterdam in 1918, created model housing estates, setting an example which has been followed with decided benefit. One can appreciate the need for mathematical order in town planning as in the work of Cornelis van Eesteren (*b.* 1897), appointed city planner to Amsterdam in 1929.

In many forms of industrial production the use of a basic geometric system of design is of manifest importance. The theories of De Stijl enabled Gerrit Rietveld (*b.* 1888) to relate the design of house and furniture on rational lines. What is notable in all these respects is that this Dutch movement spread beyond national boundaries and engaged the efforts of artists elsewhere, especially in Germany where van Doesburg's propagandist zeal was influential and Oud's contributions to the architectural exhibitions of the 1920's made a strong impression.

Like other developments of modern art, De Stijl was a compound of the visionary and the practical. Its visionary side is most remarkably represented by Mondrian in painting and Georges Vantongerloo (*b.* 1886) in three-dimensional construction. For both, it might be said, a process of thought was more important than the finished work of art. Vantongerloo especially has pursued the aim of "making thought visible". After some paintings, which made the characteristic De Stijl use of horizontals and verticals, and some sculptural constructions which applied the same method to work in three dimensions, he branched out on his own into the production of shapes in plexiglass and wire which are a kind of comment on the progress of science, of no practical utility but often with a beauty of form like that of a jewel and with an appeal to the imagination rather like that of the projects of the experimental scientist. Parallel elements of the visionary and the practical are to be found in the "Constructivism" and "Suprematism" which were a Russian contribution to modern art and in the vastly influential German school of design, the Bauhaus, or "House of Construction".

CHAPTER VIII

THE RUSSIAN PHASE OF EXPERIMENT

It is useful to remember from time to time that the development of modern art, while following threads of reasoning which concerned art alone, was not unaffected by the social and political history which was also in the making. The observer will already have noticed how the quickening speed of the century, the opening vista of the age of internal combustion and mechanical transport, directed the efforts of the Italian Futurists. So tremendous an event as the war of 1914–18 was not simply an interruption in the careers of artists but one which produced an emphatic reaction. In some it aroused a hopeful mood, in others one of bitterness and pessimism, and in both cases the mood found expression in the tasks which artists set themselves. The hopeful mood in Russia, after the collapse of the Tsarist régime in 1917 and the establishment of Bolshevik rule, resulted in an intensified desire to start afresh and to create an art which, in being revolutionary in form and ideas, might be thought the necessary accompaniment of political and social revolution.

Prior to 1914 there had been signs of a desire to recover and restore a native tradition in Russian painting. The *World of Art*, a review conducted by Serge Diaghilev and Alexandre Benois from 1899 to 1904, had played a leading part in this endeavour. A native Russian tradition, however, was not so much that of picture painting as practised in the West but of the bright colour of folk art and the rigid abstractions of icon painting. The delight in colour which was to inspire the gorgeous productions of the Russian Ballet under Diaghilev's direction, finding its pre-war expression in the designs of Léon Bakst (1866–1924), perhaps helps to account for the prompt Russian response to the Post-Impressionist and Fauve French painting in which colour was a dominant factor. Considering how slow patrons were elsewhere in appreciating such works-the prompt sympathy of the wealthy Moscow merchants with the art of Matisse and others (forming what is now one of the world's most brilliant collec, tions of modern painting) is the more noteworthy.

In the account of German painting (p. 45), the leading part played by two Russians, Wassily Kandinsky and Alexei von Jawlensky, has already been noticed. In Russia itself there was a swift progress towards abstract art which can be studied in the work of Kasimir Malevich (1878–1935). The son of a bailiff on a Russian country estate, he studied art at Kief and Moscow and was much impressed by the first exhibitions of Fauvist painting held in Moscow in 1907 and 1908. The style of his painting changed quickly from brilliantly coloured scenes of peasant life in the Fauvist manner to paintings in the Cubist-Futurist style of which *An Englishman in Moscow* (1914) (Pl. 40) is an example. Yet various influences, not least, perhaps, a Russian tendency to push ideas to their extreme, caused him to pursue an abstract course in painting from which any trace of representation had disappeared. Kandinsky had already painted his *Improvisations*, Michael Larionov (*b.* 1881) had experimented with a form of abstraction opposing light and dark rays (*Rayonism*), and by 1915 Malevich had arrived at the idea of an "absolute" art of geometric shapes and flat colour, owing nothing whatever to nature (Pl. 40). This, which he called *Suprematism*, was accompanied by fervid and not always very intelligible explanations—Plato has more clearly defined the idea of forms absolutely beautiful in themselves and not in relation to objects seen in nature. Yet Malevich's rectangular bands of colour and his famous exploit of painting white forms on white, thus indicating what subtle differences of tone the "absolute" might contain, created a grammar of abstraction which painters since have often used with varying degrees of success, though it has never ceased to inspire effort.

This is the visionary aspect of the art which, after the Revolution of 1917, seemed logically destined to "order the new world"—of Soviet Russia—according to "the new vision". The art schools, the control of teaching and galleries, were, for the time being, given over to the enthusiasts—Malevich, Kandinsky, who had found his way back to Moscow after war broke out, Vladimir Tatlin (*b.* 1885) and the artist brothers Antoine Pevsner (*b.* 1886) and

Naum Gabo (*b.* 1890 and taking the name Gabo in 1915 to avoid the confusion of two artists of the

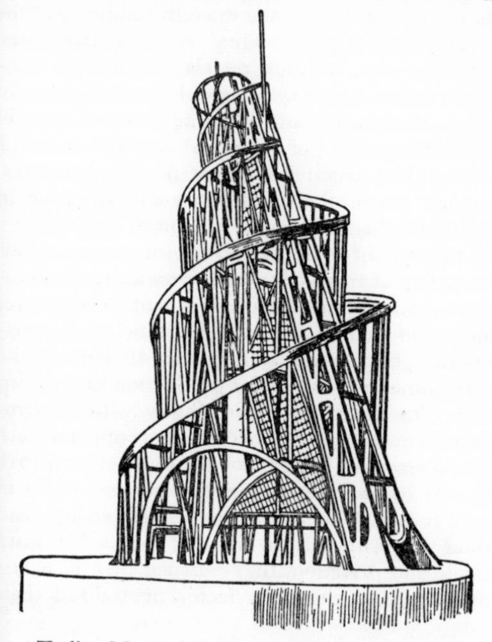

Tatlin: Monument for the Third International

ame name). They added to the experimental theory f painting that of three-dimensional construction. Pevsner and Gabo were not exactly sculptors, if culpture is taken to mean the creation of a solid form in stone, marble or wood. Their intentions were nearly related to those of the architect—if one defines architecture, in the modern fashion, as "the enclosure of space". They used untraditional materials—wire, various metals and plastic substances drawn out in systems of lines and curves of varying thicknesses and defining a given area of space with an effect of mathematical elegance. This was the "Constructivism", first practised in 1915 of which the brothers published an exposition in what they called a "Realist Manifesto" in 1920.

Tatlin sought to apply this use of new materials or new use of materials more specifically to architecture and outlined many brilliant projects for buildings of metal and glass (p. 63) which in the early post-war period seemed fantastic, though at the present time their fitness for production by modern building methods and their affinity with contemporary architectural aims become more apparent. All told, the artists of Russia took the lead between 1918 and 1921 in propagating a new expansion of art in all its forms. One must admire the energy and enthusiasm with which, in that period of grim struggle and privation, they pursued their idealistic ends; yet more than one factor neutralized their efforts.

There was a split of intention between the artists themselves. One group, of whom Malevich was the most determined, held that art must have its own independent evolution without being applied to useful and state purposes. The only socialist element in his doctrine was "to acknowledge for all the ability to create". On the other hand the new political and social order seemed to Tatlin a marvellous means of creating a new function for art in close association with the progress of mechanization and industrial production. In his view, both easel painting and purely experimental painting were out of date. What was required was the "artist-engineer" working in close consort with the technician. In so far as Russia was a peasant country, mechanically backward, this was a sensible plan for advance which received official approval for a time, yet in the long run none of the proposals commended themselves to authority. It was not only that the academic artists—who, Malevich said, "should be put on national assistance as old invalids"—raised their voice in protest. When the Soviet rulers had time from more pressing problems to consider the matter, it appeared to them that the working masses did not want and did not understand this new art. The only way to reach them was by a form of pictorial propaganda they could understand—instead of a Suprematist painting, one which pointed out either the injustices of the old régime or the material blessings to be hoped for in the new; instead of a construction in wire, an heroically conceived statue of Lenin.

The atmosphere had so far changed by 1921 that many of the *avant-garde* left Russia: Kandinsky, Pevsner, Gabo and the imaginative painter Marc Chagall, who had for a time been in charge of art at Vitebsk. Others struggled on until, at the end of the decade, "socialist realism" became the only officially tolerated form of art. This form of propaganda painting and sculpture which has remained dominant in the U.S.S.R. until the present day was the antithesis of modern art and has offered a strange contrast with Russian advances in the scientific field, being in style an enfeebled version of the academic art of the last century. A comparison between the vitality of Russian art from 1918 to the early 1920's and the mediocre or antiquated nature of much since produced can hardly fail to impress even those who have some initial bias against abstract theory. Yet the results of totalitarian censorship were not so much to crush the modern effort as to disseminate its influence farther in the West, in France and Germany. The post-1918 optimism which looked forward to a great renovation found a new centre in the German Bauhaus.

CHAPTER IX

AIMS AND INFLUENCE OF THE BAUHAUS

THE Bauhaus, organised by the architect Walter Gropius at Weimar in 1919, was a university of design which may be looked on as the end product of ideas fermenting since the time of William Morris, their basis being the need for a collective effort with a beneficial effect on life in general. The influence of Morris's ideas both in England and on the Continent had been reflected in the Art Nouveau. This is often looked on as no more than a rather exaggerated style of decoration which flourished briefly from about 1890 to 1910. Yet for the architects as distinct from the makers of jewellery, ornamental glass and other decorative objects, it was of more serious import. They conceived a union of the arts of design, with architecture occupying its old central place, and in the early years of the century there had already appeared, along with the ornamental products of the craftsman, a growing simplicity and logic of architectural construction. One of these architects, deeply impressed by the spirit of Morris, was the Belgian, Henry van de Velde, who may also be regarded as a promoter of the Bauhaus. In 1914 he proposed Walter Gropius as head of the projected Academy and School of Applied Arts at Weimar to the Duke of Saxe-Weimar, and himself designed the building to which Gropius came in 1919, after the interruption of war.

Where both parted company with Morris was in envisaging a union not solely of handicrafts, but of all the modern techniques of industrial production. Gropius's plan was radically to depart from the old-fashioned idea of an art school. He introduced a laboratory atmosphere, a basic inquiry into materials and methods. Workshop practice was substituted for such airy notions of design as prevailed in the old schools of painting and drawing. He caused the problem of design for machine and mass production to be tackled with a sense of purpose and fitness previously lacking.

It is only necessary to look back on the fumbling and inconclusive history of the schools of design in 19th-century England, instituted with the same purpose of linking art with industry but with no real conception of how it should be effected, to realize the practical importance of the venture. The Bauhaus taught architecture, interior design, painting, sculpture, photography, design for theatre, ballet and film, pottery, metalwork, textile design, typography, graphic design, and above all functional principles which were a guide to the solution of the individual problems presented. It got down to essentials in a way that has since been enormously influential, so much so that today its methods are in use by the most enlightened and successful schools in two hemispheres. First at Weimar and then at Dessau (1925–32) it united and developed all those new tendencies in Germany, Russia and Holland which have already been described, and though industrial techniques had their large part in the curriculum, painters who had led the way were prominent on the teaching staff.

Kandinsky left Russia and joined the Bauhaus in 1922 as head of the department of mural painting. Klee conducted the school of glass painting from 1921. Renewing their association of the "Blue Rider" days they worked in close amity and produced some of their most striking paintings. A change of style is notable in the abstract paintings of Kandinsky, partly due to the influence of De Stijl

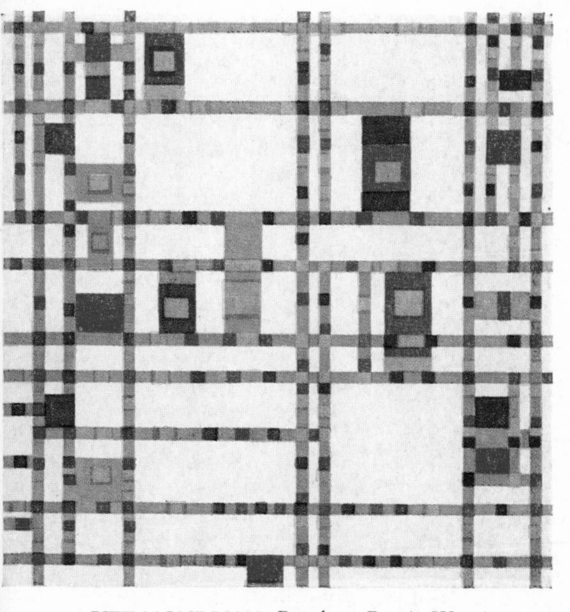

33. PIET MONDRIAN: *Broadway Boogie-Woogie*
(Collection, The Museum of Modern Art, New York)

34. ALEXEI VON JAWLENSKY: *Girl with Peonies*
(*Heydt-Museum, Wuppertal*)

35. ERNST LUDWIG KIRCHNER: *Self Portrait and Model*
(*Kunsthalle, Hamburg*)

36. EDVARD MUNCH:
Four Girls on the Bridge

(*Wallraf-Richartz-Museum, Cologne*)

37. OSKAR KOKOSCHKA: *Bride of the Winds*

(Kunstmuseum, Basle)

38. MAX BECKMANN: *Cabaret Artists*
(*City Art Gallery, Bonn*)

39. GEORGE GROSZ: *The Robbers*
(*photograph: The Arts Council of Great Britain*)

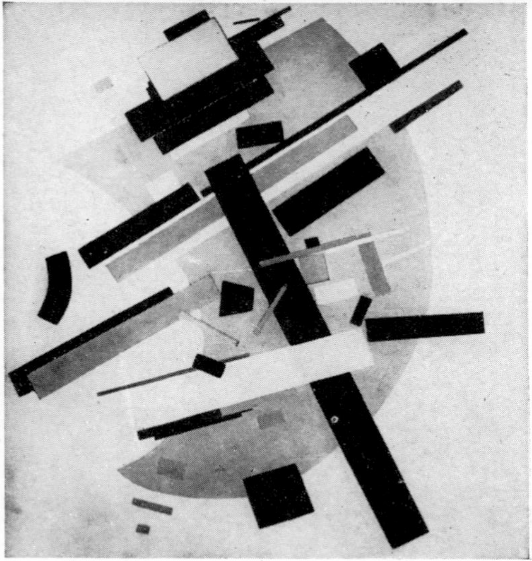

40. KASIMIR MALEVICH: (left) *An Englishman in Moscow*; (right) *Suprematism, Yellow and Black*
(*Stedelijk Museum, Amsterdam*) (*Russian Museum, Leningrad*)

41. JUAN GRIS:
Table by the Sea

(*photograph:
Marlborough Fine
Art, Ltd., London*)

42. JAMES ENSOR: *Portrait of the Painter Surrounded by Mask*
(photograph: Marlborough Fine Art, Ltd., London)

43. GEORGES ROUAULT: *Christ Mocked by Soldiers*
(*Collection, Museum of Modern Art, New York*)

44. GIORGIO DE CHIRICO: *Melancholy and Mystery of a Street*
(*Museum of Modern Art, New York,
Mr. and Mrs. Stanley R. Resor Collection*)

45. GEORGES BRAQUE: *The Pedestal Table (Le Guéridon)*
(The Phillips Collection, Washington, D.C.)

46. MAURICE DE VLAMINCK: *Landscape with Red Trees*

(Musée National d'Art Moderne, Paris)

47. MAX ERNST: *La Joie de Vivqe*

(Private Collection, London)

48. PABLO PICASSO: *Minotauromachie* (*Etching*)

(*photograph: The Arts Council of Great Britain*)

and observable in the use of more clearly defined Geometrical forms, triangle, rectangle and circle (Pl. 29). He employed them (still with something of Russian mysticism) not solely for their geometric attributes but for deep meanings—in the circle, for example, he said in 1929 "my overwhelming recognition of its inner strength and its limitless variations".

Klee allied intuition, a delightful fancy and delicate sense of humour with exploration of the range and qualities of materials, never regarding the degree of abstraction as a criterion of value but seeking always for freshness of contact between nature and mind. He used pen, watercolour, chalk and oil in varied combinations on grounds of different textures—muslin, rough canvas, gesso-covered board—but always alert for the suggestions of reality which came with their use and often pointing to them in some poetic or gaily fanciful title (Pl. 52). The Bauhaus period saw the production of many of his most charming works.

Though Malevich did not leave Russia, his pupil El Markovitch Lissitzky brought constructivist ideas to Germany which the Hungarian artist Laszlo Moholy-Nagy (1890–1941) as Bauhaus professor of metalwork, 1923–8, applied to problems of metal construction, demonstrating also the relation of abstract design to typography, the lay-out of a page or a stage or film set. The work of Josef Albers (*b.* 1888), who was in charge of craft teaching 1923–5, was also directed to the possibilities of construction in a variety of materials, wood, paper and metal, his own paintings in opaque glass being as strictly devoted to geometric ratio in the arrangement of horizontals and verticals as those of Mondrian. Other influential painter-teachers included Johannes Itten (*b.* 1888), who devised the Bauhaus basic course, and Lyonel Feininger (1871–1956), who in 1913 had exhibited with the Blue Rider group. Feininger is noted for the variant of the Cubist style which he imaginatively applied to architectural and seascape themes and seems to have been less of a pedagogue than a painter of stimulating example. In general the choice of teachers was that of painters of active intelligence whose departures from conventional picture painting made them the better equipped to deal with form and colour in other aspects.

In architecture and industrial design the Bauhaus propagated that idea of functional simplicity which, though carried to spartan limits in the 1920's, has made for a rational standard in modern design (Pl. 64). The Dessau Bauhaus designed by Gropius himself in 1925 is a classic example of modern architecture.

Yet once again modern art was to be condemned by the totalitarian state. As a liberal Germany fell under national-socialist dominance the clouds gathered about the Bauhaus. Its professors were held to be communist, degenerate or both. The school was closed down after Hitler seized power in 1933 and most of the Bauhaus masters emigrated. As in Russia, however, what seemed a destructive stroke had the reverse effect in greatly extending the

Bauhaus sphere of influence. Architecture, industrial design and art teaching gained a new impetus in the United States from those who settled there, in particular Gropius himself and his architect-successor in the Bauhaus last years, Mies van der Rohe (*b.* 1886). Moholy-Nagy became the head of a new Bauhaus at Chicago in 1937. Lyonel Feininger made his home in New York from 1936, Albers conducted courses at several American universities, Herbert Bayer (*b.* 1900), who had taught typography and advertisement design, became design adviser to American industrial corporations. The result of the dispersal was to make the Bauhaus idea an international force.

CHAPTER X

ART AS A CRITICISM OF THE AGE

In considering how the mood of art was affected by the 1914–18 war, the hopeful feeling of enthusiasm for a new epoch, in which artists sought to contribute to social development, has so far come uppermost; yet in some there was also a bitter and pessimistic reaction. It is marked by the movement called "Dada", beginning among a small group of exiles in Zürich in 1917, who assumed an attitude of irresponsibility, a sort of wild denunciation of a supposedly civilized world capable of war and slaughter on an unprecedented scale. If this made sense, they implied, it was better to be nonsensical.

Their title "Dada" ("hobby-horse") was a word picked at random from a French-German dictionary. Their nonsense expressed a disgust with politics, the social order and the forms of art identified with it.

Poets have several times been responsible for the more fanciful flights of theory in modern art—Guillaume Apollinaire and Tomasso Marinetti had already given their example—just as architects (Oud, Gropius, Mies van der Rohe) advocated a rational and practical approach. The Rumanian poet Tristan Tzara (whose real name was Rosenstock) was a leader in extravagant and "debunking" statement and performances of "noise music", poetic gibberish and visual absurdities intended to shock.

The Dadaists had no feeling for the new in art as opposed to the old; the serious purposes of Cubism and Futurism were as uncongenial to them as the older forms of professionalism. This was the post-war reaction which, after its first outburst at the Cabaret Voltaire in Zürich, made its appearance in a defeated and depressed Germany at Berlin and Cologne. Although Futurism was disowned, use was made of its aggressive methods; the noise music, the startling manifesto, the assault on convention (the German writer Richard Huelsenbeck proclaimed the intention to "drum literature into smithereens"), the incitement to pugnacious action (at one exhibition hatchets were provided, with which irritated spectators were invited to attack the outrageous exhibits). There is a strange contrast between the rowdy Dada group formed at Cologne in 1919 and the soberly constructive spirit of the Bauhaus inaugurated at Weimar in the same year.

Was Dada a temporary fever or had it any real artistic value? It lasted as a movement for only a few years. It was largely one of negations, a purge of emotions, yet as always in the study of modern art it is necessary to go not merely by manifestos and generalizations but by what individuals produced. The Dadaists numbered artists of real ability. Their seeming anarchy led in two directions—to incisive satire and to a new form of imaginative art. Outstanding in the first category is George Grosz (1893–1959), a Berliner, who began as a caricaturist, served in the 1914 war and joined the Dada movement in Berlin in 1918. Grosz concentrated his great ability as a draughtsman on a pictorial indictment of social corruption in post-war Germany: the bloated profiteers, the debased world of the night clubs, the still arrogant and brutal military caste. His drawings and water colours present a picture which is still disturbing and horrifying though with a quality of line altogether exceptional, charged with an electric vitality which seems to derive from a deeply felt hatred (Pl. 39).

This attitude in Germany was serious enough to acquire a separate description of "Neue Sachlichkeit"—the New Objectivity—not only satirical but a sombre and uncompromising view of life and human failings. Grosz is associated with this phase in the 1920's with Otto Dix (*b.* 1891), the author of ruthless portraits and a series of war etchings which are an equivalent of the anti-war novels of Remarque and Barbusse; and Max Beckmann, a remarkable painter whose pre-war Expressionism seemed to become intensified in symbolism and social meaning.

The imaginative aspect of Dada, a criticism of society only in its entire divorcement from it, is seen in the work of Kurt Schwitters (1887–1948), Max Ernst (*b.* 1891) and Jean (Hans) Arp (*b.* 1881). Schwitters, painter, sculptor and poet, is noted for his creation of collages and constructions fashioned out of odds and ends, the debris of the waste-paper basket—torn bills, travel brochures, used bus tickets, broken chair legs, decayed pieces of material. Superficially this might be dismissed as a typically irreverent Dadaist game. In fact, however, he used and pasted together these bits of rubbish with so much appreciation of colour that they become delightful to the eye and often convey the poetic thought that even what is humble, discarded or despised is capable of a beautiful transformation (Pl. 60).

Max Ernst, the founder of the Dadaist group in Cologne, obtained fantastic results by cutting up 19th-century wood engravings and pasting them together in unexpected combinations, productive of an eerie and sinister effect. With him and with Arp, however, the Dadaist phase was but the start of the exploration of the imaginative possibilities of modern art which is later to be discussed under the heading of Surrealism.

A grim commentary on Plato's thought that the free artist has no place in the politically absolute state is provided by the summary vengeance wreaked by the Nazi régime on modern German art in all its original forms, and not on the anarchism of Dada alone. From the satire of Grosz to the charming inventions of Klee and the romantic exuberance of Oskar Kokoschka, all came under the official ban after 1933. Works were expelled from public galleries. The exhibition of so-called "Degenerate Art" held in 1937 pilloried practically everything of interest and value that 20th-century German artists had produced to that date.

CHAPTER XI

THE INTERNATIONAL SCHOOL OF PARIS

PARIS, meanwhile, which had been the great launching ground of modern effort, remained its centre and inspiration, and the "School of Paris" is a term which sums up its unique position. A "school" implies some likeness of aim linking a number of artists, though Paris between the wars presents a spectacle of great diversity. It was international, artists coming there from many different countries, though there was always a strong nucleus of French artists. This, however, was not the only reason for the diversity. So swift had been the developments of the century that there was an overlap of ideas and methods derived from the several starting-points of the pre-1914 era. For instance, though Impressionism as a style belonged to the past, Pierre Bonnard, who lived until 1947, continued to pursue its direction in his paintings of landscape, interiors, nudes and still life, but with an increased and splendid richness of colour which again made him, in his later years, an inspiring influence on the young.

The artists who had initiated movements did not remain merely static emblems of this or that "ism" but showed a personal expansion of their gifts. Henri Matisse is a great artist who cannot simply be dismissed with the label "Fauve". It was his view that a painting should be soothing rather than startling; serene and without disturbing subject matter. It is reflected in his views of sunny interiors in the South of France, and in his paintings of "odalisks" (Pl. 32). As with so many of the modern masters of painting, his art extended beyond the boundaries of the picture: in design for the ballet, in exquisite outline illustrations, and in his late years with the application of his gift for colour to the design and decoration of a religious building, the Chapel of the Rosary of Vence.

Another artist who began as a Fauve, Albert Marquet (1875–1947), is noted in his later work not for aggressive colour but for a simplification of form in landscape which conveys at the same time a sense of completeness and truth to nature (Pl. 30).

There are some artists so individual as to stand quite alone. Marc Chagall (*b.* 1887), who paints lovers, peasants and toy-like villages (Pl. 28) in the spirit of the fantasy and folklore of the old Russia in which he was born, is one of these independent figures. Entirely different is the work of Amedeo Modigliani (1887–1920), who came from Italy and in the portraits and nudes (mainly painted between 1915 and 1920) exquisitely combined some modern characteristics (notably a simplifying of form derived from the sculptor Constantin Brancusi) with a sense of a human beauty of structure like that of a Botticelli (Pl. 50). Modigliani's friend, the Lithuanian artist Chaim Soutine (1894–1943) is a Bohemian figure who painted figures and still life with an intensity of feeling recalling that of Van Gogh. Maurice Utrillo (1883–1955), who invested the peeling walls and steep byways of Montmartre with a haunting character, is another artist who defies classification. Georges Rouault (1871–1958) stands alone as a painter and graphic artist of religious themes (Pl. 43), starkly and powerfully conceived. It was the freedom of Paris, the artistic excitement it generated, the presence of a multitude of lively minds and talents, and not the dominance of a particular theory, which gave a vitality to work produced there.

Perhaps the most remarkable instance is to be found in Pablo Picasso, who represents for many people all that the School of Paris stands for. He has made probably a greater impact on the public mind than any other modern artist, arousing both controversy and an undiscriminating idolatry. He is unequalled in versatility, as painter, draughtsman, etcher, lithographer, sculptor and designer of ceramics. Not only has he explored all kinds and combinations of media, but his immensely prolific output includes as wide a variety of style and subject. Some aspects of this output may appeal to the individual more, or less, than others, but his powers as a draughtsman do not admit of two opinions and his restless inventiveness reflects the variety of modern art from Cubism to Surrealism.

It is probably not at all hard for most people to understand and appreciate his paintings as a young man in the first decade of the century—the pictures of sad and yet dignified figures of poverty of his "Blue Period", about 1904, the paintings of circus performers of the "Rose Period" which followed after; or such a charming picture of childhood as *Le Gourmet* (Pl. 19). The part he played in the invention of Cubism, which has already been described, was undoubtedly a release of tremendous force which might be likened to the splitting of the atom—as witness the effect it has been possible to trace on the work of artists far and wide. It may help in following the complex variety of his subsequent work if it is considered in two aspects. First, as an extension of the early phase of Cubism, that is, breaking down the appearance of things into their components and reassembling them with striking effect. Instances are those "double-heads" in which profile and front face simultaneously appear. Often the effect is a repellent distortion—and yet in such a compound of featural character as that of his *Woman Weeping* the emotional result marvellously justifies the means.

The process extends to all sorts of art in the past—as in the series of paintings which takes to pieces and reassembles the details of Velazquez's great composition, *Las Meniñas*, executed with great virtuosity, though the result contains little of Velazquez and all of Picasso. It is typical of him to take up a theme and not leave it until he has seen it in every kind of permutation, light on dark, dark on light, now in one grouping, now in another, as in the many brilliant variations of his series of paintings of pigeons seen at a sunny window in the South of France.

What may disturb the observer in the process of analysis which takes reality to pieces, is its being destructive rather than constructive in the fashion of the Old Masters. The human sympathy and the sense of a profound reality given by the Velazquez do not survive in the variations on it. This, as we have already seen, is the essential sacrifice Cubism made to open up a new world of visual exploration.

The extension of Cubism, however, is only one side of Picasso's art. He is capable at will of a return to entire directness of representation in a painting or drawing and with this goes a variation of mood which is a continual surprise. His humour is a quality not to be overlooked, a humour which enables him to create, rather sardonically, a mythological world of fauns, satyrs and nymphs or to find endless possiblities of satirical amusement in the aspect and relation of artists—pompous, wizened, aged, short-sighted—and their models. Then again —and here indeed he seems a Spaniard akin to

Goya—he uses the symbolism of the bullfight, evoking a sense of the strange and sinister, for example in his etching the *Minotauromachie* (Pl. 48). A ferocious distortion appears in some of the work, produced during the German occupation of France, with often unpalatable results. Yet a like bitterness produced one of his most memorable works, the *Guernica* (Pl. 51), incited by the wanton bombing of a Spanish village during the Spanish civil war. A huge wall painting, virtually in black and white, now in the Museum of Modern Art, New York, it makes use of the bullfight symbolism and other symbols of not entirely clear significance; but its purport is unmistakable, it is like a cry of human agony. No modern work has more piercingly conveyed tragedy.

If one needed a reminder that the value of art is individual and is not summed up by classification in movements, none could be more apt than that provided by a comparison between Picasso and Braque. Close together originally in the adventure of Cubism, they diverge in an extraordinary fashion. Picasso is expansive, many-faceted, Braque concentrated and even conservative in effort. Cubism freed him from the conventional use of scientific perspective but only to apply him more sedulously to the representation of space and the intimate relation of objects in a given area—the guitar, peach, pipe, table, familiar features of the Cubist still life to which he remained devoted (Pl. 45). His pictorial excursions outside his studio were few but the studio itself provided all the material for masterpieces of his later years. In them he was able to give a magically heightened sense of reality and space even though everything is brought forward to lie two-dimensionally on the canvas. In these two eminent artists, both of long and continuously fruitful life, the individualism of the School of Paris is strikingly seen, though once again, in the period between the wars, a new movement came into being which, at least in intention, made a fresh union among artists: the movement called Surrealism.

CHAPTER XII

IMAGINATIVE AND FANTASTIC ART

SURREALISM was, in a way, as much a reaction from the course modern art had hitherto pursued as modern art itself had been from conventional 19th-century painting. It respected none of those aesthetic preoccupations with form and colour which had stemmed from the work of Cézanne. It reintroduced subject matter as a factor of decided importance. It was a revolt of the imagination from all discipline and restraint, a delight in the marvellous, the excessive, the irrational, the mysterious, the poetic. It raised one of those issues which are never entirely settled, the old opposition of "Classic" and "Romantic", in an up-to-date guise, as between the pursuit of a formal and geometric order and the free indulgence of the mind, even—or perhaps especially—in its most fantastic expression.

Like Futurism and Dadaism it was not confined to painters but was the scheme of poets who wished for a release of the mind from the restrictions imposed on it by the training and habitudes of modern life. The title, implying "more than reality", was first used by Guillaume Apollinaire, describing a play he wrote in 1917 as a *drame surréaliste*. It was taken up by André Breton, the French poet and theorist, who defined it as "pure psychic automatism, by which it is intended to express, whether verbally or in writing or in any other way, the real process of thought. Thought's dictation, free from any control by the reason, independent of any aesthetic or moral preoccupation."

The first Surrealist Manifesto in which this definition appeared was issued in 1924, only a few years after the sensational outbursts of Dadaism, in German cities, in Paris and New York. The movement was indeed a continuation of Dadaism, using similar shock tactics, equally opposed to all the normal curriculum of organized society, against "art" from a belief that what was so called did not really express truth of feeling. It was, however, no longer merely a fevered reaction to the war but an active attempt to explore the workings of instinct and intuition and of states of being, as in dreams, when the conscious reason is temporarily suspended. The Surrealists were much inspired by the researches of Freud into the psychology of dreams and by the idea of creating a semblance or illustration of the dream state by placing in relation incongruous and unexpected images and inducing a like feeling of suspense and tension.

Like the Dadaists they had no constructive and specifically "modern" intention. The Surrealist state of mind was one which might become manifest at any time and anywhere, independent of existing conditions in the real world. It is an interesting aspect of the movement that it sought for and named historical precursors in both literature and painting. Literature gave such examples as the fantastic novel by Huysmans, *A Rebours*, the *Chants de Maldoror* by Isidore Ducasse, which suggested the strangely compelling effect of unlikely images placed in association, and that unique dream excursion, Lewis Carroll's *Alice in Wonderland.* In painting it was possible to point to the 15th-century Flemish artist Hieronymus Bosch as a Surrealist Old Master. His fantastic paintings were as full of sex symbolism as the Freudian interpretation of a dream, of fascinating nightmare creatures which seemed to have sprung into weird life out of inanimate matter.

The operations of pure instinct could be studied, and were already being studied, when Surrealism came into being, from several points of view. One discovery of the century was the art of children, a spontaneous product before the age of adolescence brought with it more conscious effort and imposed adult disciplines; brilliant in colour and design and perhaps a phase in which the inherited memory of the child re-enacted the history of primitive art. Another discovery was that of the instinctive painting of the untrained and sometimes unlettered adult, the modern "primitive", living in his or her own dream world. The most illustrious example was the "Douanier" Rousseau (Pl. 18). In one painting he set a nude figure on a couch in the depth of an imaginary jungle conjured up from his memory of the French military expedition to Mexico—a characteristically Surrealist approach. Other and lesser discoveries of works by farm labourers, charwomen and simple craftsmen, especially in France and the United States, seemed to well from a store of expressive energy often under-estimated by those of professional accomplishment.

Yet a richer and more varied series of imaginative works than the naive products of instinct preceded Surrealism. There was James Ensor (1860–1949) in Belgium who developed a highly personal imaginative art towards the end of the last century. Living over a souvenir and curio shop in Ostend, filled with carnival masks (Pl. 42), sea shells and grotesqueries, he gave a weird life in his paintings to these objects and his masks and skeletons in uncanny assemblage often suggest an affinity with Bosch and the elder Pieter Brueghel in his more fantastic mood. Closer to the Surrealists, and even for a while a member of the group, though pictorially a precursor in date as well as spirit, was the Italian artist Giorgio de Chirico (*b.* 1888). Like most modern painters, he found an early stimulus in Paris, and between 1911 and 1915 began to produce those architectural visions of Italy full of nostalgic reverie and a dreamlike atmosphere of suspense which are among the most original products of the age.

His work runs directly counter to that of his Italian Futurist contemporaries in its contemplation of the past, statues and arcades throwing long shadows from a setting sun, though it is Surrealist in its incongruities—a locomotive for instance appearing in the same picture as an antique statue. His *Melancholy and Mystery of a Street* (Museum of Modern Art, New York) (Pl. 44), painted in 1914, is one of the masterpieces of this architectural series. In other series of paintings he depicts, with fantastic effect, lay figures with featureless egg-shaped heads, which one might imagine as the actors in some strange tragic play; and still lifes which by placing objects unexpectedly together give them an unusual vividness. This was a kind of painting he called "metaphysical", the Italian painter Carlo Carrà (*b.* 1881), who had previously been one of the Futurists, joining with him in 1917 and working along the same lines.

Other painters, without being definitely part of the movement, have been to some extent akin to Surrealists in their fanciful expression. Marc Chagall shows this kinship in his paintings of lovers soaring and swooping ecstatically through the air in defiance of the laws of gravity; Klee also, who "taking a line for a walk", in his phrase, could cause it to evolve into the vision of a fantastic city.

In what is more specifically called Surrealism

there is no one characteristic style unless one regards as typical a sharp definition of outline which may be assumed to convey the uncanny sharpness of some dream images. This is notable in the productions of Salvador Dali (*b.* 1904), who has called his paintings "hand-made photography" and professed a wish to achieve the smoothness of finish and minuteness of detail of a Pre-Raphaelite. Always desirous of shocking (an intended Surrealist objective), he has achieved this aim in various ways: with gruesome painted detail and such extravaganzas as the "limp watches" of his *The Persistence of Memory*, 1931; the film in which he collaborated with Luis Bunuel, *Un Chien Andalou*, the decaying corpse of a donkey on a grand piano appearing in one of the scenes that horrified the audience; the design for a ballet in which trees were represented by female torsos on which birds nested; and even fantastic jewellery (including ear-clips in the shape of telephone receivers).

Though the sensationalism of Dali has tended to establish him in the public mind as the arch-Surrealist, his jesting vein was regarded with some suspicion by Breton and others as a cheapening of the movement and for some critics the suspicion has not been allayed by the religious subjects to which he has turned since 1950, *Le Christ* (Glasgow Art Gallery), *St James of Compostella* (Beaverbrook Gallery, Fredericton) (Pl. 55) and others. There were Surrealist jests by others. The fur-lined teacup shown at the International Surrealist Exhibition of 1936 may be supposed to reflect a contempt for rational and commonplace utility. Marcel Duchamp's gesture of exhibiting industrially manufactured objects, what he called, 'ready-mades'', as personal inventions derides the solemnity of art exhibitions. In all seriousness, however, the Surrealist practice of displaying (often with some minor fanciful addition) and calling attention to "found objects"—a curiously formed tree-root or some odd fragment of mechanism for instance—had the effect of opening many eyes to a wider range of interest in the visible world than it was usual to perceive. The "found object" has probably had as great an influence on the outlook of later artists as Surrealist painting.

The painting is very varied. Sometimes it is the creation of imaginary and grotesque forms. The strange birds devised by Max Ernst, the amoeba-like shapes which float across a limitless plain of Yves Tanguy (1900–55), the ferocious battles of insects conceived by André Masson (*b.* 1896), the dance of rudimentary figures in gay colours by Joan Miró (*b.* 1893) (Pl. 54), are examples. There are fantasies of unworkable machinery such as Francis Picabia (1878–1953) constructed. Other painters have sought to illustrate the dream state, the Belgian artist Paul Delvaux (*b.* 1898), for instance, making many variations of the not uncommon dream in which nude figures appear among others fully clothed, all wrapped unconcernedly in hallucination. There is René Magritte (*b.* 1898), who has specialized in the art of pictorial metaphor, that is to say not merely imagining a likeness in one thing to another but actually painting it as the imagined form. The smoke of a fire becomes in thought the smoke of a locomotive which he sees issuing from an ordinary fireplace painted with great precision.

Surrealism flourished in the 1930's and in any definite form came to an end with the outbreak of war in 1939. Just as in some degree it reflected the disturbance set up by the earlier war, so also its disquieting character seems to contain some foreboding of what was to come. Some critics have expressed the view that quite apart from extraneous events it was bound to fail and disappear by its insistence on what was merely bizarre and its scant regard for the beauty of painting. Yet movements are of less importance and usually of shorter life than the individuals associated with them. Max Ernst (Pl. 47) is one who continued to increase in imaginative power long after Surrealist theory had ceased to be an active issue. In several ways the influence of Surrealism has remained operative until the present day.

On sculpture its effect has been considerable, which is rather surprising since sculpture was not a prime consideration with its promoters. In this respect the "found object" had a special significance. It drew the attention of sculptors to processes of growth and change in nature as they might be exemplified for instance by a pebble smoothed, hollowed and fissured by the constant action of the elements. Thus Jean Arp, the French sculptor, graphic artist and poet, one of the founders of the Dadaist movement in 1916 and later an active

Surrealist, has sought to convey something of nature's process of form-making in works of sculpture of an abstract kind. The great modern sculptor Henry Moore found a similar inspiration in these aspects of natural form which had not been seriously examined until Surrealism pointed them out.

It also suggested that a bronze or a carving was not necessarily a human figure of ideal physique but could be treated with something of the painter's freedom. One result of this is to be seen in the work of the Swiss artist Alberto Giacometti (*b.* 1901), who after studying under the exponent of a modern classicism, Bourdelle, became a Surrealist adherent in the 1930's and has since produced a strangely impressive statuary of exaggerated length and thinness. The idea of a mysterious or "magic" presence, not entirely human, has animated a modern school of English sculptors, notable among them being Kenneth Armitage (*b.* 1916) and Lynn Chadwick (*b.* 1914). In painting Surrealism exerted an influence of special importance in both England and the United States, which is brought out by a short general survey of the progress of modern art in both countries.

CHAPTER XIII

MODERN INFLUENCES IN ENGLAND

SEVERAL factors contributed to place England on the outer perimeter of modern art. The fact of being an island and the insular outlook thus fostered is one factor. Though Constable and Turner were great pioneers, a sort of iron curtain seems to have dropped between the island and the Continent in the period which followed. The Victorian painters lived in their own cosy world secure in the patronage of the wealthy middle class which delighted in the subject pictures they produced. Impressionism was suspiciously viewed from a far distance and Post-Impressionism, introduced by the critic Roger Fry in the celebrated exhibition of 1910–11 at the Grafton Galleries, was so unfamiliar as to seem outrageous. The love of a pictorial story, of scenes of everyday life observantly painted, and an unventuresome attitude to form and colour as such were characteristics which seemed deeply ingrained at the beginning of the 20th century.

In consequence, when an interest in what was being produced across the Channel began to awaken it seemed inevitable that England should not participate fully but follow behind in a belated and tentative fashion. Was it necessary to follow at all? Possibly not, though it is evident that the Victorian tradition had come to an end with the Victorian age which had supported it. A full history of 20th-century English painting would include artists of merit who have been little affected if at all by the modern developments of ideas and technique. Stanley Spencer (1892–1959), entirely local and with the personal feeling for religious expression which appears in his *The Resurrection*, is an outstanding example. Walter Richard Sickert (1860–1942) is a brilliant artist who has had great influence in England but remained aloof from the new developments of the century.

Yet the seeds of modern art as it had flourished abroad were scattered and took root here and there with admirable result. There is the provincial but delightful Post-Impressionist school of the Camden Town Group formed in 1911, variously applying the lessons learned from Cézanne, Gauguin and Van Gogh to English landscape and London scenes. Spencer Frederick Gore, Harold Gilman and Robert Bevan are especially notable in this group for a sense of colour quickened by the Continental masters. Generally speaking, English painting has suffered from the lack of those associations of artists where ideas are freely exchanged. The Camden Town Group, brought together by the vigorous personality of Walter Sickert, showed the value of this interchange.

Mention has already been made of the Cubist-Futurist influence in England in the pre-1914 years, this time not belated but exactly contemporary. The work of Wyndham Lewis, C. R. W. Nevinson,

Edward Wadsworth and W. P. Roberts reflects the dynamic and mechanistic spirit of Cubism and Futurism with considerable effect. Nevinson was not so powerful an artist as Léger but one can see a like train of thought in his dynamic paintings of war on the Western Front. Together with those of Paul Nash they constitute an impressive picture of the nature of modern war in which modern technique played an essential part. The French Fauve movement found an English disciple in Matthew Smith who studied in Paris and spent a brief time in the short-lived art school of Henri Matisse. The Fauve freedom of colour was instrumental in releasing the gorgeous flood of colour which is to be appreciated in the nudes and flower and still-life paintings of his maturity. Both the Cubist still life and the system of abstract design cultivated by the De Stijl painters of Holland gained an English adherent in Ben Nicholson (*b.* 1894). For many years a solitary practitioner of this abstract art in England, he is now recognized as one of its best exponents. No other artist has made pure geometric proportion so satisfying to the eye. An exquisite sense of colour and line characterize his paintings and reliefs (Pl. 57).

Yet in spite of these exceptional individual achievements English artists until the 1930's were somewhat out of their element with modern art, or perhaps it would be more accurate to say that the brilliance of the School of Paris was to many somewhat daunting. In this respect the Surrealist movement wrought a great change of attitude. Opposing formal aesthetic discipline and encouraging freedom of expression, it found a response which the example of Cézanne had failed to elicit. In a sense Surrealism was a Romantic movement and a Romantic element has always been strong in English art. Many of its most remarkable contributions to modern art have been made between the mid 1930's and the present day. To some artists Surrealism suggested new meanings and unexplored possibilities in natural form. Paul Nash found in it a release of a naturally poetic imagination which had previously been subordinated to a more formal approach to pictorial design. The "found object" became for him an element of mysterious beauty in landscape, strangely carved boulders and stones being set amid familiar downland, adding to it a feeling of the fantastic and primeval (Pl. 57).

Henry Moore (*b.* 1898) is one of those great artists who are capable of absorbing impressions from a number of different sources and making use of them in entirely individual fashion, but Surrealism is certainly to be counted among them. Aztec and Mayan sculpture, the Romanesque carvings of churches in his native Yorkshire, aspects of the work of Picasso, all provided their stimulus, but important in his development also was that relation between the sculpture of nature and the sculpture of art to which the Surrealist "found object" pointed. Of his mature works, the "Three-piece" reclining figure of 1962 (Pl. 59), in which the figure motif contains a weathered grandeur recalling that of Stonehenge, may be cited.

Pictorially the work of Graham Sutherland (*b.* 1903) shows in an especially interesting way the merging of a natively English romantic feeling for landscape with the imaginative freedom encouraged by Surrealism. As a young graphic artist he was a follower of Samuel Palmer, that disciple of William Blake who early in the 19th century had given to an apple tree in blossom, a billowing cloud, even the lichen on the roof of a Kentish barn, an intense value which came from the poetic ardour of his scrutiny. A like scrutiny in Sutherland was not so much diverted from nature as intensified by the Surrealist influence. He arrived at a turning-point in his career when, like many other modern painters, he no longer found it possible to paint a landscape scene imitatively (Pl. 49). Yet this was less an impasse than the discovery that the essence of form was equally to be found in the natural detail as in the scenic view, in a small stone as in a mountain; moreover that the detail could take on an emotional meaning, as in the tortured forms of the gnarled and dead branches of a tree, or the spikes of a thorn bush. The art of Sutherland has expanded in several directions, in paintings which investigate the strangeness of both vegetable and animal form—of bat, toad, grasshopper as well as thorn, gorse and vine; in wartime comment on the weird destruction wrought by bombing; in religious painting and design; in purely fanciful constructions, half natural and half machine-like, which come nearest to the Surrealist grotesque of the Continental artists and in striking portraits (Pl. 58). In all, his is one of the most original achievements of English art in a recent phase.

The horrific element in Surrealism was a starting-point for the work of one of the most powerful of modern painters of the present post-war age, Francis Bacon (*b.* 1910). No other artist is capable of giving the same macabre thrill as he does in his adaptations of Velazquez's portrait of Pope Innocent X (Pl. 62) with their gruesome changes of expression, and in his studies of an animal and distorted humanity. Is it necessary, the observer may ask, to paint so much that is ugly and disturbing? The answer must be that artists are free to express the truth as they see it or conceive it, and that Bacon's unprepossessing picture of life is not lacking in truth may be gathered from the effect it exerts on the feelings, a little like that of Goya's pessimistic paintings in old age of eerie grimaces in beings from whom all idealization has been removed.

CHAPTER XIV

THE RISE OF MODERN ART IN THE UNITED STATES

ON the whole, and for various reasons, the United States was more receptive to the art of continental Europe than England had been. There was a traditional link with Paris and a predisposition to new, or at least anti-Victorian, ideas of which James McNeill Whistler had given signal proof in the

1870's, while American collectors were prompt and enthusiastic in appreciation and purchase of French Impressionist painting. Paris was the training ground of American artists in the early 20th century and a pioneer modern influence can be seen in the art of the watercolourist John Marin (1870–1953), who made a brilliant abstract simplification of landscape paintings of New York and the New England coast. The vast array of modern works from Cézanne to Picasso and Marcel Duchamp in the Armory Show held in New York in 1913 made a deep impression, though a considerable time had still to elapse before modern art was entirely assimilated. The effort to create a national art on the basis of subject directed many talented painters to the realistic representation of the "American scene", still more emphatically local in the "Regionalism" of the 1930's, in which style as distinct from subject had only a subsidiary and not a characteristically modern part.

A complete survey of American painting from the 1930's to the present day would show a very wide range of effort, including for instance such a minutely descriptive study of local character as the *American Gothic* of Grant Wood (1892–1942), depicting a farmer and his wife against the background of their old-fashioned homestead, and the minutely detailed paintings of contemporary life by Andrew Wyeth (*b.* 1917); but if we are to follow the main course of modern art, the rise of an abstract school becomes a main factor to consider. It brings into view an aspect of Surrealism distinct from its dream imagery and fantasy: a reliance on expression in the form most nearly approximating to André Breton's definition of "automatism"—that produced without the control of reason. It suggested a form of abstract art which was not based on calculated geometrical proportions but was free of all restraint and came from the unconscious. The painter was now completely absorbed in the act of painting and the intensity of sensation that might be supposed to result.

What is known as "abstract expressionism" had already made its appearance in Europe. The Spanish painter Oscar Dominguez, the French painter Jean Fautrier (*b.* 1897), the German painter Wolfgang Schulze (Wols) (1913–51), had all experimented with painting in which form was no longer organic and recognizable but like the movement of atoms, a kind of cellular structure into which any substance might be scientifically resolved. In America the trend developed into what is known as "action painting". It was stimulated by the presence of French artists of the *avant-garde* who had come to America as refugees from the German occupation of France in the Second World War, and in particular by the Surrealist André Masson. It became dominant and an influence in Europe in the 1950's.

Jackson Pollock (1912–56) has come to stand internationally for the whole movement. He began with paintings in which a vehement distortion showed traces of his study of Picasso, Miró and Masson. From them he proceeded to painting from which all figurative association was excluded. His method has been described (in a way that would easily lend itself to caricature) as a purely haphazard process—the streaking of paint over a canvas stretched on the floor, and the seemingly random distribution of dribbles of sand, nails and pieces of glass in the mass of pigment. His own words give some inkling of what he was trying to do: not to convey personal emotions like the German Expressionists but to create a living substance. "When I am *in* my painting, I'm not aware of what I'm doing. It is only after a sort of 'get acquainted' period that I see what I have been about. I have no fears about making changes, destroying the image, etc., because the painting has a life of its own."

The observer may take this as a standard in appreciation and, vague as it is, it does point to a vitality which cannot be overlooked. Some of Pollock's large canvases, in addition, show a vibrant harmony which indicates a more conscious control of technique than his ideas might suggest. Yet he is only one of a considerable number of American painters who have devoted themselves to an "all-out" freedom of effort. They include Willem de Kooning (*b.* 1904), Mark Rothko (*b.* 1903), Adolph Gottlieb (*b.* 1903), Clyfford Still (*b.* 1904) and Franz Kline (1910–62), each with a personality of style, though sharing some general characteristics.

To appreciate the characteristics of American painting it is necessary to remember that the United States has two seaboards, Atlantic and Pacific. On the one side it looks towards Europe, on the other to the Far East. Thus while New York was an obvious meeting point for European and American art, there was on the other side of the continent a tendency to take a special interest in the arts of China and Japan and particularly in Oriental painting and its calligraphic nature—its "beauty of handwriting". Mark Tobey (Pl. 53) (*b.*1890) is the outstanding representative of the latter tendency, much influenced by study in the East of the brush-work of the Oriental painter-poets. In his earlier paintings he creates an abstract pattern from the aspect of a city street by night with its flashing signs and moving crowds, or from the throng of a street market, but these in course of time are transformed into an often intricate web of lines and strokes which may be looked on as a form of calligraphy. These works are usually on quite a small scale, relying on their delicacy of treatment, containing also some element of Oriental philosophy as well as tecnnique, that is to say, inviting the observer to a spirit of contemplation into which the material world does not intrude. They can be contrasted with works by other American artists executed on a very large scale, concentrating effect with a massive physical impact, the pictorial sensation in an intensely simplified form.

The geographical distinction, however, is only a rough one. Adolph Gottlieb combines this forceful impact with the use of symbols or signs that have some of the quality of handwriting. The large paintings by Mark Rothko of uneven rectangular patches, subtly merging one with another, are capable of inducing a state of unwordly meditation —if, that is, the observer is ready to enter into the spirit in which they were produced and not mentally to oppose some different conception of what painting is for. As far as the effect on artists is concerned, the "new American painting" has been a force in recent years, though in both hemispheres, with or without direct interchange and connection, a similar trend is to be seen.

CHAPTER XV

FIGURATIVE AND NON-FIGURATIVE ART SINCE THE 1940's

THE notes on the exhibition of paintings from the Musée d'Art Moderne, Paris, held in London in 1957 included the following remark: "Most of the younger artists have turned to abstract or non-figurative painting. This is a fact, reflected in the Museum's collection, that no amount of prejudice against this kind of painting can disregard. The limits of non-figuration are, in the painter's eyes, outweighed by its enormous possibilities, which the detractors often fail to recognize." It is indeed a remarkable thing that each manifestation of modern art in the last half-century, from Cubism to Surrealism, has eventually arrived at an abstract conclusion, whatever its initial intention may have been and in spite of the example given by certain

49. GRAHAM SUTHERLAND: *Entrance to a Lane*
(*Tate Gallery, London*)

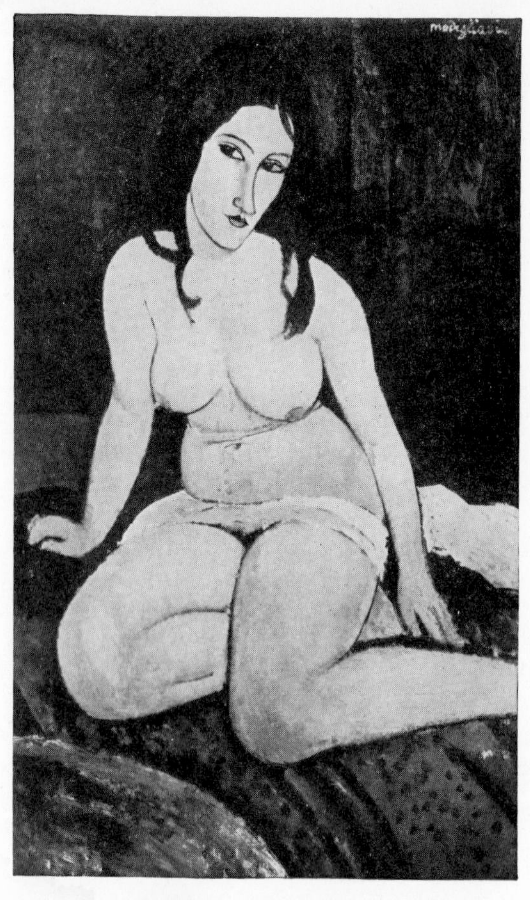

50. AMEDEO MODIGLIANI: *Seated Nude*
(*Koninklijk Museum voor Schone Kunsten, Antwerp*)

51. PABLO PICASSO: *Guernica*
(*The Museum of Modern Art, New York, on extended loan from the artist*)

52. PAUL KLEE: *Seven over the Roofs*
(*Sonja Henie—Niels Onstad Collection*)

53. MARK TOBEY: *Autumn Field*
(*The Johnson Collection, U.S.A.*)

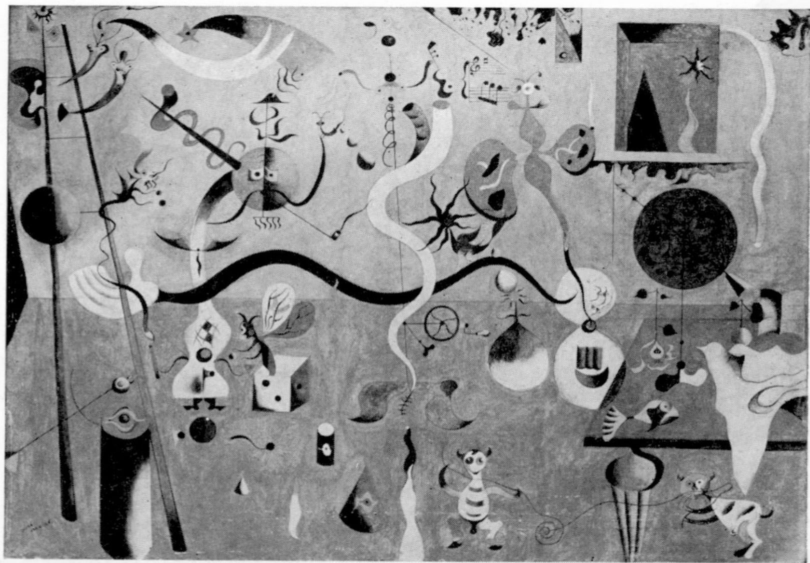

54. JOAN MIRÓ: *Carnival of Harlequin*

(*Albright-Knox Art Gallery, Buffalo, U.S.A.*)

55. SALVADOR DALI: *St. James of Compostella*
(Beaverbrook Art Gallery, Fredericton, N.B., Canada, The Sir James Dunn Foundation)

56. ALEXANDER CALDER: *Mobile: Red Feather on Black Cross*

(Private U.S. Collection)

57. BEN NICHOLSON: *Dust Blue*
(*Joseph Pulitzer Jr., St. Louis, U.S.A.*)

58. GRAHAM SUTHERLAND: *Somerset Maugham*
(*Tate Gallery, London*)

HENRY MOORE: *Three-piece Reclining Figure*
(*photograph: Marlborough Fine Art, Ltd., London*)

59. PAUL NASH: *Monster Field*
(*Durban Museum and Art Gallery, South Africa*)

60. KURT SCHWITTERS: *Dadaistic Collage*, 1920
(*Ernst Schwitters*, A.R.P.S.)

61. NICOLAS DE STAEL: *Etude de Paysage*

(*Tate Gallery London*)

62. FRANCIS BACON: *Pope with Fan Canopy*
(*photograph: Marlborough Fine Art, Ltd., London*)

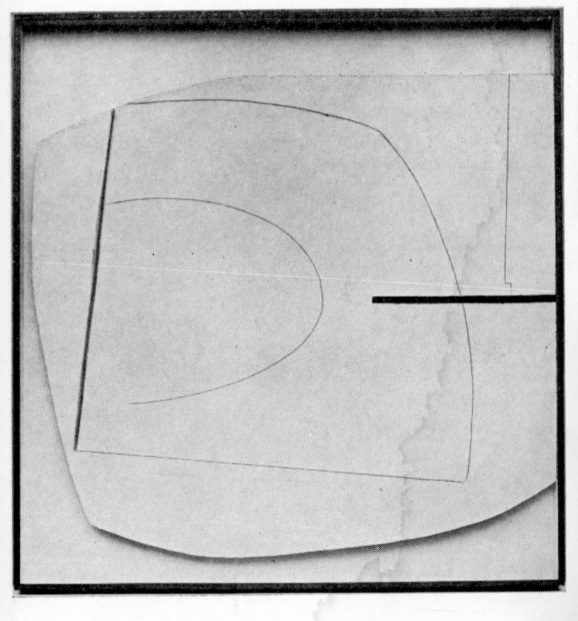

63. VICTOR PASMORE: *Linear Motif in Black and White*
(*photograph: Marlborough Fine Art, Ltd., London*)

64. *Examples showing the affinity of modern display and design to present day art forms.* (Above): *a display at the Design Centre, London.* (Below): *an Executive Office, designed by Henry Dreyfuss, in the American Banking Trust Building, New York.*

(*photographs:* The Council of Industrial Design, London)

individual masters. Picasso, for example, whatever distortions he may have used, has always been a painter of human beings, animals, birds, landscape, and natural objects, yet the Cubist and Surrealist movements with which he is associated eventually produced non-figurative results and, contrary to what one might expect, he had no direct influence on a younger generation of artists in France. It might be assumed that forces were at work independently of individuals, shaping the century's art, sending it into directions parallel with the advances of a mechanized civilization, the speculations of science and the nature of city life, the growing network of communications linking nations and making for a similarity in their products. What is beyond doubt is the rise of an international abstract art, in which there is no essential difference between the products of one country and another, though much individual variety.

At first view this may seem a confused and disordered spectacle, but when it is examined with an eye to classification, consistent patterns begin to appear. There is first the abstraction with a mathematical basis of which the later work of Kandinsky, the squares of Malevich, the rectangles of Mondrian, the geometrically conceived paintings and reliefs of Ben Nicholson, are examples. A number of artists are still working on these lines, some seeking effect by large and simple shapes of definite outline. This has come to be denoted by the term "hard edge", the work of the American artist Ellsworth Kelly (*b.* 1923) giving an example.

In contrast is the painting which deliberately makes use of the seeming accident—the trickles of fluid paint, for instance, with which Sam Francis produces an abstract design. This is to be associated with the other kinds of free or informal abstraction which are variously called expressionist and "action" painting. France, England, America, Germany, all give their examples. The "writing" or calligraphy of Mark Tobey has its European equivalents in the feathery strokes of a painting by Hans Hartung (*b.* 1904), and the linear "sign-writing" of Georges Mathieu (*b.* 1922).

There is the abstraction which has evolved from landscape or still life and still retains a suggestion of its origin as in the work of the English painters Peter Lanyon (*b.* 1918) and William Scott (*b.* 1913). One of the most interesting developments of abstract painting is to be found in the work of Nicolas de Staël (1914–55), who contrived in a number of paintings to combine the sensation given by an actual place with a purity of colour and simplicity of form which might alternatively be appreciated for their own intrinsic values (Pl. 61).

The practice of producing hybrid works, first seen in the collage of the Cubists and exploited by artists such as Kurt Schwitters, has continued until the present day, artists making use of wood, metal, paint, moulded canvas and granular substances in varied combinations with the intention sometimes of drawing notice to arresting qualities of surface and texture, and sometimes of creating an imaginative effect. Jean Dubuffet (*b.* 1901), for instance, causes fantastic figures and gardens to emerge from arrangements of dried and pressed leaves and plants.

Other artists have contemplated the possibilities of setting abstract products in motion, thus creating a changing repertoire of optical effects. Marcel Duchamp made this experiment with what he termed "Rotorreliefs". The dance of rudimentary forms which Miró suggests on canvas is turned into three dimensions by Alexander Calder (*b.* 1898) in his "mobiles", those exquisitely balanced abstract structures of painted metal which move with a touch or breath of air in graceful and varying relation (Pl. 56).

In contrast to the advance of abstract art there have been attempts to reintroduce realism. In England, the Euston Road School, formed in the late 1930's as a teaching school but eventually becoming in a more general sense a school of thought and style, was a reaction against the dominance of abstract theory, advocating that the artist should paint what he saw and holding that everyday life still had plenty of inspiration to give the painter. A leading figure was Victor Pasmore (*b.* 1908), who has painted some of the most delightful English pictures of the century, in a style which may be called Impressionist, in that atmospheric colour was an Impressionist quality.

It is a commentary, however, on the accumulated force of modern ideas of art that so sensitive and excellent a painter should, from about 1950 onwards, abandon the painting of landscape or figure for a non-figurative art both in painting and three-dimensional construction. In effect he has taken up the thread left by the architects and designers of De Stijl and the Bauhaus, viewing the work of the abstract designer as a necessary complement to the architectural planning of today and design in its more practical aspect.

A consequence of the Second World War in France was an austere realism which can be appreciated in the work of Francis Gruber (1912–48) and others, though this movement seems to have produced no lasting effect. There are scattered instances in modern painting of social realism, that is, painting with a critical comment to make or imply on the condition of society, often with the aim of revealing some shortcoming or error. The paintings by the American artist Ben Shahn (*b.* 1898) which bleakly detail the unfortunate history of Sacco and Vanzetti are notable, as also the paintings of proletarian life by the Italian artist Renato Guttuso (*b.* 1912).

While, in contrast to work of this kind, there is a strong trend towards internationalism, it is also to be remarked that in this century there have come into being two remarkable national schools, those of Mexico and Australia. They enable the observer clearly to appreciate the difference between being national and international in art. The difference is largely one of subject matter. One may speculatively find some trace of what is called national character in abstract or non-figurative art but it will only be slight or an imprecise matter of opinion, like what remains of the English love of landscape in the free abstract paintings of English artists of today. Yet there is nothing that can be called Canadian in the luscious "maps" of thickly applied colour by Jean Paul Riopelle (*b.* 1924); or French in the massive dark forms which Pierre Soulages (*b.* 1919) sets in an imaginary space; or Russian in the sheer charm of colour of an abstract composition by Serge Poliakoff (*b.* 1906); or Dutch in that fury of paint in which an image takes shape by Karel Appel (*b.* 1921). Jackson Pollock is responsible for the dictum that there is no such thing as American painting—"just as the idea of a purely American mathematics or physics would seem absurd". Though the analogy is dubious in that painting, unlike mathematics, contains a variable element of feeling, there is a measure of truth in this if one chooses to isolate the application of paint from an objective interest in the visible world. On the other hand the national schools of the past quite definitely indicate that there is such a thing as French, Italian, German, Dutch or English painting, characteristically national when artists are most concerned with their local environment.

Environment and national development have had a special importance in both Mexican and Australian art. The Mexican school of mural painting was a unique growth bound up with the prolonged struggle for democratic rights, its productions being mainly intended to instil a sense of history and national unity. Subject matter—the life of the pre-Columbian Indians, the Spanish conquest, the work of the native population under Spanish rule, the subsequent struggles against corruption and dictatorship—was the essential feature of this art, at once propagandist and educational. Of the three outstanding masters, Diego Rivera (1886–1957), José Clemente Orozco (1883–1949) and Alfaro Siqueiros (*b.* 1898), Rivera has given the most complete picture of popular life, Orozco a dramatic conception of human fate and torment, Siqueiros a fiery expression of the revolutionary spirit. Modern art in Europe played some part in their formation. Diego Rivera passed through a Cubist phase in Paris. Siqueiros brings something of the dynamic zest of Futurism to his university wall decorations in Mexico City, yet style plays a secondary part to subject. In its intensely national character Mexican mural art belongs to its own soil.

No less dramatic and exceptional is the birth of a national school of painting in Australia, a phenomenon of the post-war period. In spite of a natural bent for painting which showed itself in the late 19th century and early 20th, it was not until the 1940's that Australian artists looked at their land with an independent vision. Two factors in particular contributed to a new outlook. An exhibition of modern European art in 1939 stimulated in a number of artists a sense of artistic freedom. During the war period following, with the mobility it entailed for the defence of the continent, artists also saw far more of the country than ever before. Painting was one way of understanding it, in addition to signalizing a national maturity. Sidney Nolan (*b.* 1917), Russell Drysdale (*b.* 1912) and

Arthur Boyd (*b.* 1920) may be singled out in the brilliant number who mark the emergence of a school. Nolan has introduced us to the lunar craters, the red arid rocks, of the empty central regions; to those little outposts—hotel, store, farm, the Victorian details of a ramshackle architecture in quaintly dramatic contrast to the surrounding vastness. He has given visual life to history and legend, the epic of discovery, the exploits of a bushranger. Drysdale and Boyd in their respective ways convey the primeval mystery of landscape and aboriginal life. Without forming conventions of style they and others have used the modern intensification of colour and emphasis of form in a distinctive fashion which can be recognized as Australian.

Yet as elsewhere the younger painters have not been content to confine themselves to local subjects. Abstract art has claimed its devotees, and there are signs that Australian art is turning from the national to the international phase which seems to overleap all boundaries and leave no part of the world untouched.

A species of new representational art has, however, made its appearance in both the United States and England in the guise of what has become known as "pop art"—a kind of vernacular which borrows the popular imagery of modern life as it appears on the advertisement hoardings, in the photographs of movie stars in film magazines, the comic strip, gaudy labels, cheap souvenirs and so on. Presented in a different context, together with an added framework of painting and drawing, they become a light and mildly satirical comment on the world of everyday, as in the work of Larry Rivers (*b.* 1923), Peter Blake (*b.* 1932) and David Hockney (*b.* 1937). The use of borrowed material in unexpected relationships is not in itself new—as we have seen, it was a device of the Dadaist Schwitters—but it is brought up to date by Peter Blake in a very entertaining fashion. David Hockney indicates in some works, for example his *Second Marriage*, that the outlook represented, not merely relying on adventitious borrowings, is capable of developing into a more complete kind of story picture. It is, however, too early to say how far this movement in general is anything more than an entertaining bypath. On the whole it must be confessed that figurative art has yet to re-attain a weight and seriousness of effort which will rival the vitality of abstract painting since the last war.

CHAPTER XVI

WAYS OF LOOKING AT MODERN ART

THE story of modern art, one of long preparation but finally of sweeping onrush and dramatic change, raises a number of questions for the observer. There has been a growing difference between picture painting as practised by the old European masters, a sort of window bounded by a picture frame through which one views a piece of reality, and painting not in this sense imitative but constituting an object with a life of its own. Does this indicate a general decline in the ability to draw and paint a scene, a figure, a portrait, a realistic still life with the impressive effect that continues to delight us in the Old Masters?

This is demonstrably not so—or not necessarily so. To take an example, Victor Pasmore has painted figures and landscapes with an admirable combination of realistic skill and feeling. If, then, he has diverted his attention to geometric constructions and abstract shapes, what we have to recognize is no lack of ability to do anything else but a change of aim (Pl. 63). Another very talented English artist, Rodrigo Moynihan (*b.* 1910), has shown himself capable of a *tour-de-force* of portrait composition—in his group of the professors of the Royal College of Art—yet again he has diverted his manifest abilities to informal abstract painting.

There are two ways of regarding these and similar changes of aim. It may be said that painting has at last gained a freedom comparable with that of poetry or music and that this represents a definite advance, the disuse of subject matter being the removal of an alien or irrelevant element which enables painting to be appreciated in a purer form. Or it may be said that art was due for an overhaul of its means and techniques and that in due course the explorations of recent times will result in artists going back refreshed to the study of nature temporarily in abeyance. A cycle of departure and return of this kind has not been unknown in the past—as witness the evolution of Italian painting from its early Byzantine phase to the achievements of the Renaissance.

In either case it is desirable for the observer to consider works impartially in relation to their aim and quality, just as we look for separate merits in Duccio and Michelangelo, without complaint that the early Sienese painter lacks the anatomical mastery of the great Florentine. It is easier to do so of course when we have a certain perspective of time such as we already possess in viewing the works of the Post-Impressionists. The paintings of Van Gogh at which people once looked askance are now assimilated in modern experience to the extent that they have become popular. It is not so easy when we come to more recent paintings in which representation has a smaller part or even no part at all.

Let us take a really difficult case, a painting by an "abstract expressionist". Is it more than a haphazard distribution of colours on a canvas, without meaning for anyone other than the painter? It depends on the quality of the painter as an individual. Some works of this kind are exciting in that they seem to touch a nerve, to exert a power of suggestion, to convey vitality, though what the artist has to communicate is here least exactly defined. It must be granted that the results are sometimes open to criticism from several points of view. There are merely imitative products of the international style; ephemeral products, destined for early oblivion once the novelty has worn off, works which all too plainly show a lack of craftsmanship and an impermanence of material. Unlimited freedom has its drawbacks as well as its advantages, yet the significant fact remains that the work of certain individuals stands out as original. Study and comparison in non-representational as in representational art will eventually distinguish for you what is of value.

But modern art, as this brief account may have indicated, takes many forms. One may as a matter of personal taste prefer some to others, yet the whole evolution is a wonderful aspect of the age. An art has come into being as characteristic of our time as that of any period in the past. Sometimes it reflects the doubts, anxieties and difficulties of the time as well as its hopes, but it is alive with the life of the 20th century.

A GLOSSARY OF TERMS

Abstract Art. Painting or sculpture which does not attempt a complete imitation of objects or effects in nature but uses form and colour selectively and for their own sake. All art is in some degree abstract, in the sense of being selective, but the logical conclusion and extreme belong especially to the 20th century. It has two main forms, in works which begin with the study of nature but arrive at an abstract result by a process of elimination, and in works which contain no element of representation but are conceived entirely in terms of geometrical figures or free expression. The latter are more accurately described as "non-figurative" or "non-representational". The first completely non-figurative paintings were produced around 1910.

Abstract Expressionism. An entirely free use of paint which relies on the operation of instinct or the "unconscious" for its effect and not on some predetermined aim systematically pursued. It was a product of Surrealism and an international development of the period following the Second World War. It is closely related to the "action painting" of American artists.

Action Painting. Term invented by an American critic, Harold Rosenberg, for a form of painting developed in the United States which attached importance to the physical action of freely applying paint and the advantage that could be taken of the fortuitous effects thus produced. Its principal representative was Jackson Pollock.

Art Nouveau. The "new art" of around 1890–1910, one aspect of which was an extravagant use of curvature in various forms of decorative design. As such it was short-lived but it was a first suggestion of that association between architecture, painting, sculpture and craft which was later more systematically developed by the De Stijl group in Holland and the Bauhaus in Germany.

Automatism. In art that which is spontaneously produced without the conscious control of the mind. It was a main item in the Surrealist theory that work so produced was nearer to the truth of feeling than that governed by conventional habits of thought and training.

Collage (Fr. "pasting" or "sticking"). The use of varied materials—wallpaper, fabric, printed matter—stuck on a ground to form a composition or part of a composition together with an element of painting or drawing. First practised by the Cubist painters, its aim was to give a variety of surface texture and also to provide a stimulating contrast between painted surface and material substance. It has since been widely employed in modern art, sometimes as a kind of intermediate art form between painting and sculptural relief.

Constructivism. Art movement originating in Russia in the early years of the Bolshevik Revolution. Taking some suggestions from the Cubist practice of collage, it was applied to the construction of three-dimensional objects in metal, wire and glass, partly with a view to a useful application in architecture but also for the sake of the effects thus obtained as a form of design akin to sculpture. It is exemplified by the work of Naum Gabo and Antoine Pevsner.

Cubism. New treatment of form and space in painting, developing from the idea that a geometric structure was the base of all form in nature. It was evolved by Pablo Picasso and Georges Braque between 1906 and 1914. It is usual to divide it into two periods: analytic, about 1909–12, when surface appearance was replaced by the study of structure and the simultaneous presentation of different aspects of the same subject, and synthetic, a more decorative use of the latter device from 1912 onwards, a principal product being the Cubist still life. As a style it was taken up by a number of artists and has since been very influential on the whole course of modern art.

Dada. A movement which began as a protest against war in 1916 by a group of poets and painters in Zürich. They expressed disillusion by guying all the traditions of culture and staging exhibitions designed to offend conventional taste, these being held after the war in Germany and France. A more purposeful outcome of the movement was Surrealism.

Divisionism. Term describing a technical development from the Impressionist method of translating light and shade into colour. It was pursued by Georges Seurat in the 1880's. It entailed the scientific combination of primary or spectrum colours in a mosaic of dots or patches, fusing into various tones when seen at a distance but giving a heightened and vibrant colour effect. It is also known as Pointillism from the French *pointiller*—to dot or stipple. Its ultimate effect was to encourage the use of brilliant and definite colour, as in the work of Van Gogh.

Expressionism. Term referring to the forms of art which aim to convey something of the artist himself and his feelings as a person, more especially those of a deeply emotional kind. The Norwegian painter Edvard Munch and Van Gogh, who conveyed an intense fervour in swirling forms and a tumult of colour, had a great influence on the growth of the Expressionist movement in Germany before and after the First World War.

Found object. Term applied to what were once regarded as curiosities or freaks of nature, likenesses to animal form for instance appearing in tree roots. The Surrealist painters delighted in these natural fantasies, sometimes exhibiting them with a slight addition to indicate what they had seen in them. The useful result was to extend the modern artist's view of form in nature.

Frottage. French word for "rubbing", a technique employed by Max Ernst similar to that used in taking rubbings of church brasses, the grain or pattern of an object or surface being brought out through a sheet of paper over which a pencil is passed. The result could be used as an element of texture in the practice of collage.

Futurism. Italian art movement launched by the poet Marinetti in 1909. It sought to interpret the spirit of the 20th Century in terms of movement, speed and machine forms. It stemmed from Cubism, though differing from it in the deliberate attempt to bring art and life into association.

Impressionism. The great effort of French 19th century painters to interpret the beauty of light by means of colour, a necessary prologue to modern art. A continuous evolution leads from the work of the Impressionists, Monet and Pissarro, to that of Seurat, Cézanne, Gauguin and Van Gogh. The work of Monet's last period, showing different effects of light on a pool of water-lilies, has a later parallel in the phase of modern art which has been called Abstract Impressionism.

Neo-Impressionism. Term invented to describe the systematization of the Impressionist use of colour by Seurat and others. See also "Divisionism".

New objectivity. Translation of the German phase "Neue Sachlichkeit", a sense of reality which in Germany took the form of a clinical view of society. It is represented by the satirical drawings of George Grosz and the paintings of Otto Dix and Max Beckmann.

Neo-plasticism. Title of a manifesto published in Paris in 1920 by the Dutch De Stijl group of artists, proposing a close co-operation between the visual arts and defినding the term as a means of extracting a fundamental origin from the apparent chaos of nature.

Non-figurative art. See "Abstract Art".

Object trouvé. See "Found Object".

Orphism. One of several classifications of Cubism invented by Guillaume Apollinaire. It refers to its more abstract form as represented by the work of Robert Delaunay and the Czech painter Franz Kupka, its principal feature being the use of colours in related effect for their own sake and without reference to recognizable objects.

Pop art. Term roughly describing a tendency, notable in the 1960's, to comment pictorially on modern life by making use of the popular imagery of advertisement, photographs of film idols, curiosities of design, scribbled slogans, etc., as ingredients of painting and collage. It somewhat resembles, in its assemblage of oddments, the Dadaism of around 1920 brought up to date and has likewise a somewhat derisive character.

Post-Impressionism. Name given to those developments in modern painting which followed and grew out of the Impressionist movement; represented by the work of Seurat, Cézanne, Van Gogh and Gauguin. It can be approximately dated between the 1880's and the advent of Fauvism and Cubism in the first decade of the present century. The great artists mentioned not only modified or reacted against Impressionism but set an altered course for the 20th century in form, colour and emotional expression.

Primitivism. Modern artists have been interested in the work of artists in primitive forms of society for two reasons, for its elementary vigour of form (as in African sculpture), a counterbalance to the over-sophisticated tendencies of Europe, and as an aspect of the instinctive expression which has been a strong factor in modern art. The art of the naïve and untrained artist of recent or present times, the "modern primitive", has been a resulting discovery.

Purism. Term sometimes used in a general sense to indicate a simplifying process designed to rid art of unnecessary detail and irrelevant associations. It could be illustrated by the way in which the sculptor Brancusi conveys flight in a simplified bird-like form. More specifically it was the aim propagated by the architect Le Corbusier and the painter Ozenfant and set out in the work on which they collaborated in 1918, *Après le Cubisme*. To purify Cubism, they held it necessary to use strictly geometrical elements. The aim was related to that of the Dutch De Stijl movement.

Rayonism. A form of abstract painting based on the contrast of light and dark rays, devised by the Russian painter and ballet designer Michael Larionov—one of the first products of abstract theory.

Simultaneity. Term first applied by the chemist Chevreul to the related effect of different colours seen at the same time side by side. It was adapted by the painter Delaunay to describe his aims. It also applies to the Cubist and Futurist practice of showing different aspects of the same form in one painting.

Social realism. Art which takes a critical view of life, often with the aim of drawing attention to some shortcoming of society.

Socialist realism. To be distinguished from Social Realism; a form of pictorial propaganda, officially sponsored, as in U.S.S.R.

Suprematism. Russian form of abstract art, based on geometrical form, devised by the painter and theorist Malevich around 1912. It has had much influence on abstract painting since.

Surrealism. Next to Cubism the most influential movement of the 20th century, based on the idea of giving free play to the imagination and relying much, at least in theory, on the operations of the subconscious mind. It first developed in Paris in the 1920's as a more constructive sequel to the Dadaist movement and gathered adherents and influence in the 1930's, the International Exhibition of 1936 being a notable landmark. It has taken various forms and made a lasting impression in Europe, England and the United States.

Vorticism. A variant on Cubist and Futurist ideas to which a number of artists in England subscribed around 1914, the leading spirit being Wyndham Lewis.

BIOGRAPHICAL NOTES

Albers, Joseph (*b.* 1888). German painter specializing in abstract geometrical design, concentrating on one figure as in his *Homage to the Square*, and using only two or three colours. He was a successful teacher at the Bauhaus, Dessau, 1925–33. He subsequently settled in U.S.A. and was head of the Department of Design, Yale University, 1950–9.

Apollinaire, Guillaume (1880–1918). French poet and writer on art, of partly Polish origin, a strong influence on modern art in his defence and theoretic exposition of Cubism. His *Les Peintres Cubistes* was published in 1913.

Appel, Karel (*b.* 1921). Dutch painter working in France in a forceful Expressionist manner. He was co-founder in 1948 of an experimental group, COBRA, with adherents in Holland, Denmark and Belgium. The title of the group was formed from the initial letters of the capital cities represented—*C*openhagen, *B*russels and *A*msterdam.

Arp, Jean (*b.* 1888). French sculptor and abstract designer, one of the founders of the Dadaist movement at Zürich in 1916, later an adherent of Surrealism. His work includes collages and sculpture in which flowing forms of irregular shape create striking effect.

Bacon, Francis (*b.* 1910). English painter whose work, stemming from Surrealism, is noted for its dramatic and macabre character. His adaptations of Velazquez's *Pope Innocent X*, of a Van Gogh self-portrait and photography in various forms (e.g. facial expression taken from Eisenstein's film *Potemkin*), show a remarkable, if gruesome, imagination.

Balla, Giacomo (*b.* 1871). Italian Futurist painter noted for his attempts to represent movement (as in his *Dog on a Leash*, Museum of Modern Art, New York) and dynamic effects of speed. From the 1920's onwards he turned towards a more traditional form of painting.

Beckmann, Max (1884–1950). German painter, an outstanding figure in the Expressionist movement. He represents the spirit of the New Objectivity in Germany after the 1914–18 war, bleak in its view of life. Dry and hard in execution, his work shows great imaginative power in group composition. Dismissed from his professorship at Frankfurt under the Nazi régime, he emigrated and from 1947 worked in U.S.A.

Bevan, Robert (1865–1925). English Post-Impressionist painter, a member of the Camden Town Group, influenced by Gauguin. He applied Post-Impressionist colour and design to views of London with distinguished effect.

Boccioni, Umberto (1882–1916). Italian Futurist painter and sculptor, a principal exponent of the Futurist aim of expressing dynamic energy.

Bonnard, Pierre (1867–1947). French painter, lithographer and designer. His early works are mostly scenes of Paris and Parisian life with a feeling for decorative pattern derived from the Japanese print. His later landscapes, interiors, nudes and still life concentrated on values of pure painting and colour in a way which inspired younger painters.

Bosch, Hieronymus (active 1480, *d.* 1516). Netherlandish painter, the most fantastically inventive of artists, as in the *Garden of Terrestrial Delights* (Prado, Madrid), claimed by the Surrealists as a great precursor.

Boyd, Arthur (*b.* 1920). Australian painter, one of the artists who have created a distinct Australian school. His works interpret the life and landscape of the continent in a distinctive and imaginative fashion, a well-known series being that of the *Half-caste Bride*.

Brancusi, Constantin (1876–1957). Rumanian sculptor, famous for his beautifully simplified treatment of bird and fish forms—refined abstractions, the influence of which can be seen in the art of Modigliani.

Braque, Georges (1882–1963). One of the greatest modern painters. For a time a follower of the Fauve group, he made some of the first Cubist pictures after studying Cézanne, developing what is known as "analytic Cubism" in association with Pablo Picasso, about 1910. Subsequently he pursued a way of his own, mainly in still life, making interesting use of *papiers collés*, pieces of wallpaper, etc., combined with painting and introducing effects of graining and marbling (suggested by early experience in a decorating firm) giving much variety of texture. His eminence, however, mainly derives from a sense of space and relation between objects of which the paintings of his studio interior executed in the 1950s were the final magnificent result.

Calder, Alexander (*b.* 1898). American artist, originally trained as an engineer, famous for the invention of the "mobile", a product intermediary between painting and sculpture, a moveable abstraction with components of painted metal.

Carrà, Carlo (*b.* 1881). Italian painter, one of the founders of the Futurist movement in 1910. He later broke away from Futurism and in 1917 joined with de Chirico in the imaginative style of painting they called "metaphysical". From 1921 he reverted to a more realistic style.

Cézanne, Paul (1839–1906). French, Post-Impressionist painter, one of the great formative influences on modern painting. His early works were influenced by Delacroix and Manet. He exhibited with the Impressionists, 1874–7, but later worked in isolation at Aix, evolving a mode of pictorial structure which made a tremendous impression on a younger generation.

Chagall, Marc (*b.* 1887). Russian painter of the School of Paris. Before going to Paris in 1910 he designed stage sets with Leon Bakst. He brought to the West a style of fantastic subject and rich colour reminiscent of old Russia, slightly affected by Cubist influence.

Chirico, Giorgio de (*b.* 1888). Italian painter, one of the most imaginative of modern artists. He studied in Athens, Munich and Paris and his work combines objects and symbols of past and present in haunting and poetic fashion. "Metaphysical" was his own term for his painting. After being associated with the Surrealists, he turned against modern art and from 1943 reverted to a more academic style of painting.

Constable, John (1776–1837). One of the greatest landscape painters, to be accounted a pioneer of modern art in his creation of a new technique for the rendering of light, with freely applied touches of broken colour, anticipating the method of the Impressionists. The Salon of 1824 in which his *Hay Wain* was exhibited, deeply impressing Delacroix and others, is a landmark in the history of 19th century French painting.

Corbusier, Le (Charles Edouard Jeanneret) (*b.* 1887). Swiss architect, painter and writer, influential advocate of an entirely modern architecture and system of town planning, also associated with the painters Léger and Ozenfant in the 1920's in propagating a "purist" art making formal use of geometrical shapes.

Dali Salvador (*b.* 1904). Spanish painter, illustrator and writer, the author of extravagant works carrying Surrealist theory to the limits of sensationalism. He has used fantastic imagery in minutely detailed painting, horrific films, exhibition display and jewellery design. In the 1950's he took to religious painting with controversial result in his *Christ on the Cross*, 1951 (Glasgow Art Gallery), and other works.

Delacroix Ferdinand-Victor-Eugène (1798–1863). Great French painter, principal figure of the Romantic movement in France but also a formative influence on modern art in the effect he exerted on French artists throughout the 19th century including Cézanne and Van Gogh, by a use of colour which was both scientific and emotional.

Delaunay, Robert (1885–1941). French painter, noted as an early exponent of abstract art. Influenced by Cubism and Futurism in paintings of Paris and the Eiffel Tower and studies of active movement of runners and football players, he also studied the abstract relationships of colours, following the lead given by the scientist Chevreul. His "colour discs" made a great impression on German painters of the Blue Rider group, about 1912.

Delvaux, Paul (*b.* 1897). Belgian Surrealist painter, who began as a student of architecture. Influenced by de Chirico and Magritte he became noted for dream-like pictures of figures, clothed and unclothed, in fanciful architectural settings.

Derain, André (1880–1954). French painter, engraver and designer, noted for his part in the Fauve movement and such brilliant early works as his series of London paintings of 1906. He was one of the first to appreciate and collect African sculpture. His later work, varied in style, was an effort to return to classic tradition.

Diaghilev, Serge (1872–1929). Impresario of Russian ballet, has a place in the history of modern art by his enlistment of modern painters to design for ballets, e.g. Picasso (*Parade*, *Le Chapeau Tricorne*) Gris, Miró, Rouault and others.

Dix, Otto (*b.* 1891). German Expressionist painter and graphic artist, associated with the New Objectivity group, his work showing the anti-war reaction and depression of Germany after 1918 and grim in character, as in his series of war etchings.

Doesburg, Theo van (1883–1931). Dutch painter and theorist, founder of the De Stijl movement and an advocate of a reformed relationship between architecture, painting and the arts of design. His ideas were related to those of Le Corbusier in France and Gropius in Germany.

Drysdale, Russell (*b.* 1912). Australian painter, leading representative of the effort since the Second World War to interpret Australian life and landscape.

Dubuffet, Jean (*b.* 1901). French painter, noted since the 1940's as an exponent of qualities to be found in "l'Art Brut"—"art in the raw" (as in primitive and child productions), also for experiment with unconventional materials, tar, putty, cement, collages of dried leaves, etc.

Duchamp, Marcel (*b.* 1887). French painter first influenced by Cubism and Futurism, noted for his *Nude descending a staircase*, 1912, showing simultaneously successive stages of movement. He later cultivated the "anti-art" attitude of the Dadaists, making use of the oddities of machine forms. He settled in U.S.A.

Dufy, Raoul (1877–1953). French painter who evolved a personal style, around 1912, from Fauve influence, gay, sketchy and brightly coloured, depicting sporting, ceremonial and theatrical occasions. He also produced mural paintings and decorative design for silks and tapestries.

Ensor, James (1860–1949). Belgian painter and etcher, noted for his fantastic figure compositions, masks and skeletons satirizing humanity. He developed his personal style in the 1880's, and anticipates much that is typical of Expressionist and Surrealist art.

Ernst, Max (*b.* 1891). German Surrealist painter. After studying philosophy in youth he turned to painting in 1913, was associated with the sensational Dada exhibitions in Cologne and later joined the Surrealist group in Paris. He developed the technique of collage, reassembling cuttings from old wood-engravings with weirdly fascinating effect. In his later work he conjures up fantastic cities and forests, making use of a spongy application of paint derived from a Spanish Surrealist, Oscar Dominguez, and known by the latter as "decalcomania".

Feininger, Lyonel (1871–1956). American-born, went to Germany in 1887 to study music but stayed to become a painter. He was associated with the Blue Rider group and taught at the Bauhaus from 1919. His work is a poetical variant of Cubism applied to paintings of sea, ships and old German cities. After the Nazi régime began he returned to U.S.A.

Fry, Roger (1886–1934). English critic and painter who introduced Post-Impressionist art to England and exerted much influence by drawing attention to purely aesthetic qualities, as in the work of Cézanne.

Gabo, Naum (*b.* 1890). Russian Constructivist sculptor and painter, who studied at Munich and there met Kandinsky and other members of the *avant-garde.* He worked in Moscow, 1917–22 developing with his brother, Antoine Pevsner, the idea of linear construction using wire, metal and glass. He designed a setting for Diaghilev's ballet *La Chatte* in 1926. He settled in U.S.A. in 1946.

Gauguin, Paul (1848–1803). One of the great Post-Impressionist painters. Influenced by Pissarro, he contributed to the Impressionist exhibitions, 1880–6 and devoted himself entirely to painting in 1883. His work has two striking phases—at Pont-Aven, Brittany, and finally in the South Seas—and marks a new departure in its boldly simplified forms and emotional colour.

Giacometti, Alberto (*b.* 1901). Swiss sculptor and painter, noted for an imaginative type of sculpture with a distinctive elongation of the figure. He settled in Paris in 1922 and was associated with the Surrealist movement.

Gilman, Harold (1876–1919). English Post-Impressionist painter of portraits, landscape and still life, influenced by Van Gogh.

Gore, Spencer Frederick (1878–1914). English Post-Impressionist painter, mainly of landscape distinguished in colour.

Gris, Juan (1887–1927). Spanish painter who settled in Paris in 1906 and took part in the Cubist movement, being noted especially for his still lifes. They show a well-defined order in which his training as an engineer and scientific turn of mind appear. He designed several décors for Diaghilev ballets.

Gropius, Walter (*b.* 1883). German-American architect, who after practising in Berlin was appointed director of the Bauhaus at Weimar in 1919 and was responsible for its remarkable progress as a school which equipped students for every form of modern design. He later became professor of architecture at Harvard University.

Grosz, George (1893–1959). German draughtsman and painter noted for his satirical and brilliant pen drawing. He studied at Dresden and Berlin, began his career as a caricaturist and after war service became a member of the Dada movement in Berlin, 1918–20, being later associated with the New Objectivity of the 1920's and pillorying the failings of German society. He settled in U.S.A. in 1933, his work being proscribed in Nazi Germany. Later works, showing abhorrence of war, lacked the artistic quality of his drawings and paintings of the 1920's.

Gruber, Francis (1912–48). French painter, who is noted for a kind of realism in which there is a mournful intensity of feeling, shown especially in works executed after the French Liberation. His *Job* (Tate Gallery) symbolizes the ordeal of an occupied country.

Guttuso, Renato (*b.* 1912). Italian painter and writer on art, leader of a social realist group, noted for pictures of contemporary Italian life, especially of the Sicilian peasantry.

Hartung, Hans (*b.* 1904). German-born painter of the School of Paris who became a French citizen in 1942. Influenced at an early stage by the *Improvisations* of Kandinsky, he has developed a personal form of non-figurative art.

Itten, Johannes (*b.* 1888). Swiss painter and teacher, the creator of a basic course at the Bauhaus where he taught 1919–23. He was Director of the School and Museum of Applied Arts at Zürich, 1938–54. His own work evolved from abstract to representational painting.

Jawlensky, Alexei von (1864–1941). Russian painter noted for figures and heads, rich in colour and with something of the stylized character of the Russian icon.

Kandinsky, Wassily (1866–1944). Russian abstract painter and theorist, who began to study painting at Munich in 1896. His early work shows French Fauve influence but in 1910 he produced the first of his non-figurative works, *Improvisations*, designed to convey a musical sensation. A leader of the Blue Rider group in Munich, he returned to Russia in the war of 1914–18 and was one of those who encouraged experiment in art in the first years of revolution. In 1921 he returned to Germany and was professor at the Bauhaus, 1922–32, his abstract painting in this period taking on a more geometrical character. He moved to Paris in 1933 from the Nazi régime, which threw out fifty-seven of his works from museums. He became a French citizen in 1939.

Kirchner, Ernst Ludwig (1880–1938). German painter and graphic artist, a leader of the Die Brücke group. Influenced by Munch and Van Gogh, he developed an art of brilliant colour akin to that of the Fauves in France, though harsher in character.

Klee, Paul (1879–1940). German-Swiss painter, one of the outstanding figures of modern art. He studied at Munich, beginning as a graphic artist, and settled in the city in 1906, becoming associated in 1911 with the Blue Rider group. A visit to Tunis in 1914 (as well as the work of Delaunay) opened his eyes to the possibilities of colour. He was appointed professor at the Bauhaus at Weimar in 1920 and spent productive years there, in close accord with Kandinsky. His reflections and researches in technique, his *Pedagogical Sketchbook*, were published in 1925. His work is characterized by a delight in the qualities of his media, a sympathy with the symbolic art of primitive peoples, and a varied inventiveness, often pointed with delicate humour in his picture titles. Dismissed by the Nazis from a post at the Düsseldorf Academy in 1933, he returned to Berne. The Nazis withdrew 102 of his works from museums in 1937.

Kline, Franz (1910–62). American painter of the abstract expressionist school, his art being characterized by bold brush strokes of calligraphic suggestion. He taught in New York and Philadelphia and his work was widely exhibited and collected in the United States.

Kokoschka, Oskar (*b.* 1886). Austrian-born painter, a vigorous and independent personality in modern art. He studied at Vienna and worked both there and at Berlin and Dresden in the early years of the century, his vehement expression in painting and opinion associating him with the German Expressionists—from whom otherwise he is somewhat apart. From 1924 onwards he travelled extensively and the rise of the Nazis, whom he outspokenly opposed, caused him to move to Prague in 1933 and thence to England in 1938. He became a naturalized British subject in 1947. He has produced memorable works in landscape, portraiture and figure composition, a Romantic masterpiece being his *Bride of the Winds* (Kunstmuseum, Basle) (Pl. 37), others being magnificent panoramic views of European cities.

Kooning, Willem de (*b.* 1904). Leading American painter of the abstract expressionist school. He was born and studied in Holland and went to U.S.A. in 1926, developing his characteristic style in the 1930's, a free and vehement handling of paint.

Leck, Bart von der (*b.* 1876). Dutch painter, a member of the De Stijl group, who used only primary colours in arrangements of strictly geometrical shapes.

Léger, Fernand (1881–1955). French painter and designer, noted for a distinctive personal style derived from Cubism and Futurism, making use of machine forms and objects derived from the industrial city background. Later he produced decoratively simplified paintings of figures—cyclists, acrobats, etc. He worked in U.S.A., 1940–5, then returned to France. His strong sense of design appeared effectively in numerous works in stained glass and mosaic. He was also a ballet and theatre designer.

Lewis, Percy, Wyndham (1884–1957). English painter and writer. Influenced by Cubist and Futurist ideas, he was the leader of the Vorticist movement of which the publication *Blast*, 1914–15, was the manifesto, advocating the use of machine forms in painting. Traces of the hard geometrical style are to be found in his many portraits and imaginative designs, though he eventually disclaimed abstract ends and the idea of progress in art.

Lissitzky, El (1890–1941). Russian painter and theorist, who pursued the ideas of geometric abstraction conceived by Malevich and carried them to Holland and Germany. He designed the gallery of abstract art in the Hanover Museum, 1925.

Macke, August (1887–1914). German painter, a member of the "Blue Rider" group at Munich. He studied art at Düsseldorf and showed a brilliant sense of colour encouraged by acquaintance with French painting and a visit to North Africa. He is noted for his park and street scenes.

Magritte, René (*b.* 1898). Belgian Surrealist painter, first inspired by the work of de Chirico, noted for a personal use of "metaphor", for example the eye, painted as a mirror in which sky and clouds are reflected.

Malevich, Kasimir (1878–1935). Russian painter, one of the first inventors of a completely non-figurative and geometrical art. He first produced boldly designed and coloured paintings of peasant life, 1908–10, then passed through a Cubist-Futurist phase before launching the abstract theory of Suprematism in 1913. His influence in Russia waned in the 1920's but continued to affect the course of art elsewhere.

Manet, Edouard (1832–3). French painter, an inspiration to the Impressionists and called "the first of modern painters" in reference to the fact that he brought new life into the method of direct painting as well as being contemporary in subject matter.

Marc, Franz (1880–1916). German painter, a leader in the "Blue Rider" group, noted for his brilliant colour and paintings of a utopian world of animal nature. He studied the work of Van Gogh and Gauguin in Paris and was later influenced by Delaunay and Cubist and Futurist ideas of construction.

Marquet, Albert (1875–1947). French painter, a friend of Matisse, one of the original members of the Fauve group, later showing an exceptional gift for conveying the essentials of a landscape scene without over-emphasis of form or colour.

Masson, André (*b.* 1896). French painter and graphic artist, a leading figure in the Surrealist movement, noted for his ability to convey a sense of feverish animation, sometimes in compositions (*Metamorphoses*) making use of insect, fish, plant and bird forms and sometimes in more abstract vein. He worked in U.S.A., 1941–5, and influenced the trend towards "action painting" and abstract expressionism.

Matisse, Henri (1869–1954). French painter, draughtsman, sculptor, lithographer and etcher, one of the most creative modern artists. He began to paint in 1890, first working on Impressionist lines. The Post-Impressionist masters gave him a new approach to colour, brilliant works shown in the Salon d'Automne in 1905 earning the title Fauve (wild beast) for him and his associates. Early Fauve works were strident in colour, e.g. *The Dance* (Leningrad), but he was later influenced by the colour harmonies of the Persian miniature, around 1910, and aimed at a luxurious refinement of effect. Figure paintings, interior scenes and still lifes exemplify it. His graphic work shows a masterly economy. Late experiments with coloured paper show a purely decorative aspect of his work. He settled at Vence in 1943 and designed an original decorative scheme for the new Dominican chapel there in 1951.

Miró, Joan (*b.* 1893). Spanish painter who studied at Barcelona and settled in Paris in 1920. First influenced by the Cubism of Picasso, he joined the Surrealist movement in 1925 and became noted for brightly coloured fantastic paintings in which abstract shapes and figures seem to move in an energetic dance. He designed costumes and décor for Diaghilev's ballet *Romeo and Juliet* (with Max Ernst), 1925, and for the Monte Carlo ballet *Jeux d'Enfants*, 1931.

Modigliani, Amedeo (1884–1920). Italian painter and sculptor who settled in Paris in 1906 and produced some of the most beautiful modern figure paintings. His interest in African sculpture suggested an elongation appearing in both paintings and sculptured heads, though in linear and plastic sense his work was reminiscent of Italian tradition.

Mondrian, Piet (1872–1944). Dutch abstract painter noted for the development of a rigidly mathematical form of painting. He studied the work of the Cubists in Paris, 1911–14, and returning to Holland was associated

extensively, painting the Queensland "outback", the desert interior and the cattle country of the Northern Territory and producing works dealing with the history and legends of early Australian days in a vivid modern style, with Surrealist undertones. Later works include a series of *Leda and the Swan*, 1960, and appropriately primitive designs for Stravinsky's *Rite of Spring*.

Nolde, Emil (1867–1956), German Expressionist painter, a member of the Die Brücke group in Dresden for a time. He began as a wood-carver but turned to painting and was influenced by the Post-Impressionists and by primitive art. His most characteristic works are religious subjects intense in colour and feeling.

Orozco, José Clemente (1883–1949). Perhaps the greatest of the modern painters of Mexico, especially in mural painting, examples of which are to be found in both Mexico and U.S.A. His principal achievements date from the 1930's, their general theme being the martyrdom and endurance of man, his murals in the Orphanage at Guadalajara and the Church of Jesus Nazareno, Mexico City, having an awe-inspiring force.

Ozenfant, Amédée (*b.* 1886). French painter and theorist, with Le Corbusier the advocate of a modified Cubism which they called "purist". After 1938 he worked and taught in U.S.A.

Pasmore, Victor (*b.* 1908). English painter, one of the founders of the Euston Road School, 1937–9, noted until the 1940's for realistic painting, especially atmospheric landscape, showing a distinguished sense of colour. Subsequently with a radical change of outlook he abandoned representation to devote himself to abstract painting and construction. As Master of Painting at Durham University from 1954, he introduced corresponding innovations in teaching.

Permeke, Constant (1886–1952). Belgian Expressionist painter, noted for powerful studies of working class and peasant life. His first important works were produced in England during the 1914–18 war, in a period of convalescence after wounds received while serving in the Belgian army.

Pevsner, Antoine (*b.* 1886). Russian-born artist of the School of Paris, who began as a painter but is mainly known for his three-dimensional constructions in plastic and metal. With his brother Naum Gabo, he evolved the theory of Constructivism in Russia, 1917–21. He settled in France in 1923 and was a member of the influential group of the 1930's devoted to abstract art—"Abstraction-Création".

Picabia, Francis (*b.* 1878). French painter whose work reflects varied aspects of modern art, from Cubism to abstraction. He formed a Dadaist group in New York in 1917, making fanciful and satirical use of machine forms.

Picasso, Pablo (*b.* 1881). Spanish-born artist of the School of Paris, a great international influence and most versatile representative of modern art, his work including mural and easel painting, sculpture, etching, aquatint, lithography, wood- and lino-cuts, illustration, design for ballet and ceramics. His work shows many changes of style and subject. Early works, around 1900, were in the *fin-de-siècle* style of Toulouse-Lautrec. The years 1901–4 were a period of austere figure painting in tones of blue; 1905–6 ("Rose period") he painted circus performers in delicate colour; 1907–9 saw the decisive change in which with Georges Braque he evolved the "new language" of Cubism. In 1912–14 he produced many Cubist still lifes, making inventive use of collage. During the 1920's he reverted to classical themes and also produced ballet designs for Diaghilev. Sinister and tragic elements appear in his work in the 1930's, influenced both by Surrealist ideas and by the political climate of the time, his *Guernica* of 1937 being a main outcome. His use of the "double image", simultaneously presenting two aspects of a head, later produced disconcerting effects of distortion. Illustrations to Buffon's *Natural History* 1942, ceramics at Villauris from 1946, paintings dissecting the work of Old Masters and many series of variations on a theme, e.g. artist and model, are aspects of his prolific later years.

Pissarro, Camille (1831–1903). Leading representative of the Impressionist movement, also important in modern art as an inspiring influence on the Post-Impressionists, Cézanne and Gauguin especially. He was associated for a time in the 1880's with the extension of Impressionist colour theory represented by the work of Seurat.

Poliakoff, Serge (*b.* 1906). Russian-born painter noted for richly coloured abstract works. He went to Paris in 1924 and studied both there and in London, subsequently working in both France and England.

Pollock, Jackson (1912–56). American abstract expressionist ("action") painter, notable for the delight he conveys in the act of painting and the advantage taken of random effects which are welded into a harmonious unity. He studied at Los Angeles and was influenced for a time by Picasso and the Surrealists, but about 1946 evolved a distinctive abstract method of his own.

Renoir, Auguste (1841–1919). French Impressionist painter, whose work in his later years shows a modern warmth and intensity of colour.

Richards, Ceri (*b.* 1903). English painter whose art developed with the abstract and Surrealist tendencies of the 1930's, noted for a poetic semi-abstract form of painting as in his variations on Debussy's musical theme "La Cathédrale Engloutie".

Riopelle, Jean-Paul (*b.* 1924). Canadian abstract painter who first studied at Montreal and was converted to free expression in paint by the Surrealist theory of André Breton, 1945, subsequently settling in Paris.

Rivera, Diego (1886–1957). Mexican painter, a principal representative of the modern Mexican school, noted for his mural paintings. A visit to Paris, where he lived from 1911–20, caused him to paint in the Cubist style, though little trace of it remained in the monumental works he began to paint in Mexico in 1922 which initiated a new phase in Mexican art. Decoratively conceived, though with a strong propagandist element, his murals give a vivid panorama of Mexican life and history.

Rivers, Larry (*b.* 1923). American painter of the New York school who uses the commonplaces of modern life—a scribbled menu, a cigarette pack, a Ford truck, for instance—in a light-hearted fashion to convey a personal impression of the world around him. His work has influenced what has been called "pop art" in England.

Roberts, William (*b.* 1895). English painter, originally a member of the Vorticist group, who has applied principles of mechanical construction to compositions illustrative of everyday life.

Rothko, Mark (*b.* 1903). Russian-born American abstract painter who reduces abstraction to an ultimate simplicity in horizontal bands of subtly related colour, impressive (as no such description can convey) when seen on a large scale.

Rouault, Georges (1871–1958). French painter, etcher and lithographer. He studied art in the atelier of Gustave Moreau where he first met Matisse, with whom he was associated for a while in the Fauve movement. His work in general, however, is noted for its sombre religious character, related in emotional quality to that of the German Expressionists. Etchings, such as his *Miserere* series, were among his most striking products.

Rousseau, Henri Julien ("le Douanier") (1844–1910). French painter, the archetype of modern primitive, who devoted himself to painting in 1884 on retirement from a small official post, producing views of Paris, portraits, imagined exotic landscapes and allegorical compositions showing a remarkable candour and originality of vision. His work was admired by the Cubist group in the early years of this century and created a modern taste for the work of the "primitive", though other discoveries have been of lesser calibre.

Russolo, Luigi (*b.* 1885). Italian painter and musician, one of the Futurist group. He invented a "sound-machine" emitting mechanical noises, a device which has since been used by others in conjunction with movable abstract constructions.

Schmidt-Rottluff, Karl (*b.* 1884). German Expressionist painter, graphic artist and sculptor. He was one of the founders of the "Die Brücke" group in Dresden and is noted for a bold style sometimes harking back to the old German woodcut, as in a series of religious prints, but also influenced by primitive art. The Nazis confiscated 608 of his works in 1937 and in 1941 he was forbidden to paint. In 1946 he became professor at the Berlin Academy.

Schwitters, Kurt (1887–1948). German painter, sculptor and poet, noted for collages and constructions made out of odds and ends. Until 1917 he was an academic painter but was subsequently associated with the Dada movement. He left Germany in 1937, his later life being spent in England.

Scott, William (*b.* 1913). English painter who has developed a simplified form of abstract painting from the "table-top" still life.

Seurat, Georges (1859–91). French painter and draughtsman, an innovator in the technique of colour known as Divisionism or Pointillism. His work departs from Impressionism in its geometrically constructed composition.

Severini, Gino (*b.* 1883). Italian painter, adherent of Futurism, first influenced by Seurat but using Cubist methods later in scenes involving movement. After the Futurist phase he turned to mural decoration in fresco and mosaic.

Shahn, Ben (*b.* 1898). American painter of social subjects, e.g. *Dreyfus*, 1931, *Sacco and Vanzetti*, 1932. He has also painted murals in U.S.A.

Sickert, Walter Richard (1860–1942). English painter, influenced by Whistler and Degas, who continued an Impressionist tradition. Though critical of Post-Impressionist art he was a stimulating influence on younger painters.

Signac, Paul (1863–1935). French painter and theorist associated with Seurat in the development of the Divisionist colour technique which he consistently pursued. His theory of colour was set out in his book *From Eugène Delacroix to Neo-Impressionism*, 1899.

Siqueiros, David Alfaro (*b.* 1898). Mexican painter and graphic artist, inspired by the Mexican revolution to produce a fervid form of mural art.

Smith, Sir Matthew (1879–1959). English painter noted for his brilliant colour, first stimulated by the example of the French Fauves and a brief period spent in the school of Henri Matisse. He did much work in France until 1939.

Soulages, Pierre (*b.* 1919). One of the leading post-war abstract painters of the School of Paris, dark and massive dolmen-like forms against a light background being characteristic of his work.

Soutine, Chaim (1894–1943). Lithuanian-born painter of the School of Paris. He settled in Paris in 1911, living in the same conditions of Bohemian privation as his friend Modigliani. In intensity of colour and handling, his portraits and still lifes have something in common with the art of Van Gogh.

Staël, Nicolas de (1914–55). Russian-born painter of the School of Paris, an outstandingly original artist of the post-war period. He settled in Paris in 1937 and developed a brilliant form of abstraction in the late 1940's. An important feature of his later work is the suggestion of landscape and figure implicit in his abstract design.

Sutherland, Graham (*b.* 1903). English painter and designer who began as etcher and engraver in a Romantic manner but developed an original style of painting in the 1930's, stimulated, like that of Paul Nash, by Surrealism. His works include the *Crucifixion*, 1946 (St Matthew, Northampton), *The Origin of the Land*, 1951 (Tate Gallery), *Portrait of Somerset Maugham*, 1949 (Tate Gallery), and Tapestry for Coventry Cathedral, 1962.

Tanguy, Yves (1900–55). French-born painter who settled in U.S.A. in 1939. He was a member of the

Surrealist group in Paris in 1925 and is noted for imaginative paintings of amoeba-like forms, minutely executed and set in spacious perspectives.

Tobey, Mark (*b.* 1890). American painter, a leading figure of the West Coast School. He travelled in the East and his work shows the influence of Oriental calligraphy, though often elaborated in intricate pattern.

Toulouse-Lautrec, Henride (1846–1901). French painter, draughtsman and lithographer, "modern" in intensity of mood and expression and abstract brilliance of graphic design.

Turner, J. M. W. (1775–1851). Great landscape painter whose work anticipates some of the most striking developments of modern art, not only in the treatment of atmospheric effect but in the abstract "colour poems" of the interiors he painted at Petworth and the "expressionist" force of his late paintings of tempestuous movement.

Utrillo, Maurice (1883–1955). French painter noted for his paintings of Montmartre. He worked originally in an Impressionist style but developed a style of his own, seen at its best in the work of 1909–14. A later development was a more naïve and brightly coloured mode of painting.

Van Gogh, Vincent (1853–1890). One of the great Post-Impressionist painters. His first paintings were dark pictures of peasant life and Dutch landscape but the work of the Impressionists' and Neo-Impressionists' made him aware of the value of colour, which he wonderfully displayed, in a short period of feverish production and in spite of grave disabilities, from 1888 to 1890 at Arles, St Rémy and Auvers-sur-l'Oise. This brilliant colour was an example to the Fauve painters and his emotional form of expression was an influence on modern art in Germany.

Vantongerloo, George (*b.* 1886). Netherlandish painter, sculptor and theorist associated with the Dutch De Stijl group. His early work consisted of rectangular constructions and geometric paintings in the style generally characteristic of the group, but he later produced a unique series of works in plexiglass which he described as studies in space and an effort to express its beauty.

Vasarely, Victor de (*b.* 1908). Hungarian painter of the School of Paris who has concentrated on optical effect, especially in black and white designs, e.g. the effect on the eye produced by black and white squares in alternation or undulating lines.

Vlaminck, Maurice de (1876–1958). French painter and writer, one of the original Fauve group. Much influenced by Van Gogh, he developed a dramatic, heavily loaded style of painting in still life and pictures of French villages.

Wadsworth, Edward (1889–1949). English painter associated with Wyndham Lewis in the pre-1914 Vorticist movement. He later specialized in the painting of marine objects in a decorative manner somewhat influenced by Surrealism.

Wood, Christopher (1901–30). English painter in a naïve manner, somewhat influenced by the School of Paris of the 1920's and also by the native Cornish primitive, Alfred Wallis. Breton coast scenes are among his best works.

INDEX

Abstract Art, 47, 101, 104–5, 112
Abstract Expressionism, 97, 112
Action Painting, 98, 112
African Sculpture, "discovery" of, 33
Albers, Josef, 69, 71, 119
American Painting, the New, 95–100
Apollinaire, Guillaume, 36, 38, 40, 72, 82, 119
Appel, Karel, 105, 119
Armitage, Kenneth, 89
Armory Show, The, 96
Arp, Jean, 74, 88, 119
Art Nouveau, 67, 113
Australian Painting, 106–7
Automatism, 82, 113

Bacon, Francis, 95, 119, Pl. 62
Bakst, Léon, 61
Balla, Giacomo, 51, 120, Pl. 24
Bauhaus, The, 66–71
Bayer, Herbert, 71
Beckmann, Max, 49, 74, 120, Pl. 38
Benois, Alexandre, 61
Bernard, Emile, 23
Bevan, Robert, 91, 120
Blake, Peter, 108
Blaue Reiter group, 45, *et seq.*
Boccioni, Umberto, 51, 52, 120
Bonnard, Pierre, 25, 76, 120
Boudin (Eugène), 5
Bosch, Hieronymus, 83, 120
Boyd, Arthur, 107, 120
Brancusi, Constantin, 77, 121
Braque, Georges, 30, 33 *et seq.*, 53, 80, 121, Pls. 20, 45
Breton, André, 82, 97
Bunuel, Luis, 86

Calder, Alexander, 103, 121, Pl. 56
Calligraphy in Painting, 99, 102
Camden Town Group, The, 91
Carrà, Carlo, 51, 85, 121
Carroll, Lewis, 83
Cézanne, Paul, 12, 13–18, 20, 32, 36, 91, 122, Pls. 5, 14, 15
Chadwick, Lynn, 89
Chagall, Marc., 65, 76, 122, Pl. 28
Chevreul, Michel-Eugène, 9, 41
Chirico, Giorgio de, 84–85, 122, Pl. 44
Cloisonnism, 23
Collage, 38–39, 102, 113
Constable, John, 2, 90, 122, Pl. 2
Constructivism, 64, 113

Corbusier, Le, 54, 122
Courbet, Gustave, 3, 5
Cross, Henri-Edmond, 11
Cubism, 31–42, 52, 113

"Dada" Movement, The, 71–73, 82, 114
Dali, Salvador, 86, 123, Pl. 55
Degas, Edgar, 5, 7, 8, Pl. 6
Delacroix, Eugène, 2, 14, 123
Delaunay, Robert, 41, 45, 123
Delvaux, Paul, 87, 123
Denis, Maurice, 25
Derain, André, 27, 28, 29, 33, 123, Pl. 17
De Stijl group, 55–59
Diaghilev, Serge, 61, 124
Die Brücke, 44–45
Dix, Otto, 73, 124
Divisionism, 9, 114
Doesburg, Theo van, 55, 58, 124
Dominguez, Oscar, 97
Drysdale, Russell, 106, 124
Dubuffet, Jean, 102, 124
Ducasse, Isidore, 83
Duchamp, Marcel, 42, 51–52, 87, 103, 124, Pl. 26
Dufy, Raoul, 30, 124, Pl. 31

Eesteren, Cornelis van, 58
England, Modern Influences in, 90–95
Ensor, James, 84, 125, Pl. 42
Ernst, Max, 39, 74, 87–88, 125, Pl. 47
Euston Road School, 103
Expressionism, 43–49, 114

Fautrier, Jean, 97
Fauves, The, 26–31
Feininger, Lyonel, 70, 125
"Found Object", The, 87, 93, 115
Francis, Sam, 102
Freud (Sigmund), 82
Friesz, Othon, 30
Frottage, 115
Fry, Roger, 53, 90, 125
Futurism, 49–54, 72, 115

Gabo, Naum, 63, 65, 125
Gauguin, Paul, 12, 18, 20, 21, 22–26, 31, 32, 33, 91, 126, Pls. 11, 12, 13
Giacometti, Alberto, 89, 126
Gilman, Harold, 91, 126
Gleizes, Albert, 41
Gonzales, José, *see* Gris
Gore, Spencer, 91, 126
Gottlieb, Adolph, 98
Gris, Juan, 39, 40, 126, Pl. 41
Gropius, Walter, 66 *et seq.*, 72, 126
Grosz, George, 73, 75, 127, Pl. 39
Gruber, Francis, 104, 127
Guttuso, Renato, 104, 127

Hartung, Hans, 102, 127
Heckel, Eric, 45
Hockney, David, 108

Huelsenbeck, Richard, 72
Huysmans, (J. K.), 83

Impressionism, 4, 5–8, 11, 115
Itten, Joannes, 70, 127

Japanese Print, The, 7, 27
Jawlensky, Alexei von, 30, 45–46, 61, 127, Pl. 34
Jongkind (J. B.), 5

Kandinsky, Wassily, 30, 45–48, 61, 65, 68, 128, Pl. 29
Kelly, Ellsworth, 101
Kirchner, Ernst Ludwig, 45, 128, Pl. 35
Klee, Paul, 45–46, 69, 85, 128, Pl. 52
Kline, Franz., 98, 129
Kokoschka, Oskar, 49, 75, 129, Pl. 37
Kooning, Willem de, 98, 129
Kupka, Franz, 116

Lanyon, Peter, 102
Larionov, Michael, 62
Laurens, Henri, 42
Leck, Bart van der, 58, 129
Léger, Fernand, 53–54, 92, 129, Pl. 23
Lewis, Percy Wyndham, 53, 91, 130, Pl. 27
Lipchitz, Jacques, 42
Lissitzky, El, 69, 130
Luce, Maximilien, 11

Macke, August, 45–46, 130
Magritte, René, 87, 130
Malevich, Kasimir, 30, 52, 61–62, 69, 101, 130, Pl. 40
Manet, Edouard, 1, 3, 4, 13, 131
Marc, Franz, 45–46, 131, Pl. 25
Marcoussis, Louis, 41
Marin, John, 96
Marinetti, Filippo Tomasso, 50, 72
Marquet, Albert, 27, 76, 131, Pl. 30
Masson, André, 87, 97, 131
Mathieu, Georges, 102
Matisse, Henri, 26–29, 61, 76, 92, 131, Pls. 21, 32
"Metaphysical" painting, 85
Metzinger, Jean, 41
Mexican School, The, 105–6
Miró, Joan, 87, 97, 103, 132, Pl. 54
"Mobiles", 103
Modigliani, Amedeo, 77, 132, Pl. 50
Moholy-Nagy, Laszlo, 69, 71
Mondrian, Piet, 57, 58, 101, 132, Pl. 33
Monet, Claude, 4, 5, 6, 7, 9, 11, 133, Pl. 3
Monticelli (Adolphe), 14
Moore, Henry, 89, 93, 133, Pl. 59
Morandi, Giorgio, 133
Morisot, Berthe, 5

Morris, William, 2, 66
Moynihan, Rodrigo, 109
Munch, Edvard, 43–44, 133, Pl. 36

Nabis, The, 25
Nash, Paul, 92, 93, 134, Pl. 59
Neo-Impressionism, 9, 115
Neo-Plasticism, 116
Nevinson, C. R. W., 53, 91, 92, 134
Nicholson, Ben, 92, 101, 134, Pl. 57
Nolan, Sidney, 106, 134
Nolde, Emil, 45, 135

Ozenfant, Amédée, 55, 135
Oud, J. J. P., 58, 72
Orozco, José Clemente, 106, 135
Orphism, 116

Palmer, Samuel, 94
Pasmore, Victor, 103, 109, 135, Pl. 63
Permeke, Constant, 49
Pevsner, Antoine, 62, 65, 136
Picabia, Francis, 87, 136
Picasso, Pablo, 33 *et seq.*, 53, 77–80, 97, 101, 136, Pls. 19, 22, 48, 51
Pissarro, Camille, 5, 7, 14, 15, 22, 137
Pointillism, 9, 11
Poliakoff, Serge, 105, 137
Pollock, Jackson, 97–98, 105, 137
"Pop Art", 107, 116
Post-Impressionist Exhibitions, 53, 90
Post-Impressionism, 8, 12–25, 116
Pre-Raphaelites, The, 1, 2
Primitive, The modern, 42
Primitivism, 117
Purism, 117

Ranson, Paul, 25
Rayonism, 62, 117
Realism, 3, 11
Regionalism, American, 96
Renoir, Auguste, 5, 7, 137
Richards, Ceri, 137
Rietveld, Gerrit, 58
Riopelle, Jean-Paul, 105, 138
Rivera, Diego, 106, 138
Rivers, Larry, 108, 138
Roberts, W. P., 92, 138
Rohe, Mies van der, 71, 72
Rothko, Mark, 98–99, 138
Rouault, Georges, 27, 77, 139, Pl. 43
Rousseau, Henri, 42, 84, 139, Pl. 18
Russian Phase of Experiment, 60–66
Russolo, Luigi, 51, 53, 139

Salon des Refusés, 4
Schmidt-Rottluff, Karl, 45, 139
School of Paris, 75–81
Schwitters, Kurt, 74, 102, 108, 139, Pl. 60
Scott, William, 102, 140
Section d'Or, 41

Sérusier, Paul, 23, 25
Seurat, Georges, 9–11, 19, 20, 140, Pls. 1, 7
Severini, Gino, 51, 140
Shahn, Ben, 104, 140
Sickert, W. R., 91, 140
Signac, Paul, 11, 140, Pl. 8
Simultaneity, 117
Siqueiros, Alfaro, 106, 140
Sisley, Alfred, 5
Smith, Sir Matthew, 31, 92, 141
Social Realism, 104, 118
Socialist Realism, 118
Soulages, Pierre, 105, 141
Soutine, Chaim, 77, 141
Spencer, Stanley, 91
Staël, Nicolas de, 102, 141, Pl. 61
Still, Clyfford, 98
Suprematism, 62, 118
Surrealism, 81 *et seq.*, 118
Sutherland, Graham, 94, 141, Pls. 49, 58
Synthetism, 23
Symbolism, 23

Tanguy, Yves, 87, 141
Tatlin, Vladimir, 62–64
Tobey, Mark, 99, 102, 142, Pl. 53
Toulouse-Lautrec, Henri de, 8, 34, 142, Pl. 6
Tzara, Tristan, 72
Turner, J. M. W., 1, 2, 90, 142, Pl. 4

Utrillo, Maurice, 77, 142

Van der Velde, Henry, 67
Van Gogh, Vincent, 12, 18–22, 26, 29, 31, 32, 43, 91, 110, 142, Pls. 9, 10, 16
Vantongerloo, Georges, 59, 143
Vasarely, Victor de, 143
Villon, Jacques, 41
Vlaminck, Maurice de, 27, 29, 33, 143, Pl. 46
Vorticism, 53, 118
Vuillard, Edouard, 25

Wadsworth, Edward, 92, 143
Whistler, James McNeill, 8, 95
Wols (Wolfgang Schulze), 97
Wood, Christopher, 143
Wood, Grant, 96
Wyeth, Andrew, 96

MODERN ART 2

CU

Painting : Collage

Style

1917 —

CONSTRUCTIVISM & SUPREMATISM (Russia)

MALEVICH (1878–1935)
GABO (1890 —)
PEVSNER (1886 —)
TATLIN (1885 —)

DE STIJL (Holland) 1917 —

VAN DOESBURG (1883–1931)
MONDRIAN (1872–1944)
Van der LECK (1876 —)

1919–1933

BAUHAUS (Germany)

KANDINSKY (1866–1944)
KLEE (1879–1940)
ALBERS (1888 —)

Architecture & Industrial Design in Europe & U.S.A.

192

L'ESPRIT N

LÉGER (18
CORBUSIER
OZENFANT

and

SCHOOL OF

PICASSO
BRAQUE
MATISSE
MODIGLIA
SOUTINE (
ROUAULT (
CHAGALL
SOULAGES
HARTUNG

INTERNATIONAL ABSTR

GEOMETRIC ABSTRACTION

NICHOLSON (1894 —)
PASMORE (1908 —)
VASARELY (1908 —)

SEMI-ABSTRACT

DE STAEL (1914–1955)

CALLIGRAPHIC

MARK TOBEY (1890 —)

AC

E

R

FIGURATIVE REVIVALS · R